Cultivating *the* Genius *of* Black Children

Other Redleaf Press Books by Debra Ren-Etta Sullivan

Learning to Lead:
Effective Leadership Skills for Teachers of Young Children
Second Edition

Learning from the Bumps in the Road:
Insights from Early Childhood Leaders
with Holly Elissa Bruno, Janet Gonzalez-Mena, and
Luis Antonio Hernandez

Redleaf Press®
www.redleafpress.org
800-423-8309

Cultivating *the* Genius *of* Black Children

STRATEGIES TO CLOSE THE ACHIEVEMENT GAP
IN THE EARLY YEARS

Debra Ren-Etta Sullivan

Published by Redleaf Press
10 Yorkton Court
St. Paul, MN 55117
www.redleafpress.org

First edition 2016
Cover design by Erin Kirk New
Cover and interior photographs by Jarkoris R. Scroggins
Interior design by Wendy Holdman
Typeset in Dante Std. and Myriad Pro.
Printed in the United States of America
23 22 21 20 19 18 17 16   1 2 3 4 5 6 7 8

Library of Congress Cataloging-in-Publication Data
Names: Sullivan, Debra Ren-Etta, author.
Title: Cultivating the genius of black children : strategies to close the
    achievement gap in the early years / Debra Ren-Etta Sullivan.
Description: First edition. | St. Paul, MN : Redleaf Press, 2016. | Includes
    bibliographical references and index.
Identifiers: LCCN 2015036080 | ISBN 9781605544052 (paperback : alk. paper)
Subjects: LCSH: African Americans—Education (Early childhood) | African
    American children—Education. | Early childhood education—Social aspects—
    United States. | Academic achievement—Social aspects—United States.
    | BISAC: EDUCATION / Preschool & Kindergarten. | EDUCATION /
    Multicultural Education. | EDUCATION / Philosophy & Social Aspects. |
    EDUCATION / Teaching Methods & Materials / General.
Classification: LCC LC2765 .S85 2016 | DDC 371.829/96073--dc23

Printed on acid-free paper

*This book is dedicated to all Black children
and the wonderful ways they light up our classrooms
and add sparkling energy to our days!*

Contents

Acknowledgments

Many, many thanks to Kyra Ostendorf and David Heath, my Redleaf team who got me started on this journey! Those early meetings really helped give shape to my ideas. Thanks also to Sara Wise for taking my millions of ideas and giving them structure! Thank you, Siobhan and Porter, for encouraging me to keep writing and for reminding me of your own early learning experiences. I also want to acknowledge Jarkoris R. Scroggins and the wonderful pictures he captured of my grandson, Aaron Michael-Scott Sullivan. Every time I see that face, I am reminded how critical it is to constantly cultivate the genius of Black children.

Introduction

BLACK CHILDREN ARE GENIUSES just waiting to show the world their exceptional intellectual ability, creativity, and originality. Of course, most children are geniuses and they are *so excited* to go to school. They can't wait to begin learning all of those wonderful things they've been dying to know. Their smiles are big, and either their little bodies can't keep still because there is so much to see and do and say *or* they sit perfectly still, not moving a muscle—just in case the mere act of breathing causes them to miss something. That was my daughter, Siobhan.

I will never forget her first day of kindergarten. Siobhan had loved preschool, but she was even more excited about starting kindergarten at "the big kids' school." She had been in the building numerous times because her two older brothers went there and I was on the School Commission. I pulled up to the curb and opened the car door for her. She jumped out, yelled, "Bye, Mom!," and took off running into the building. I stood there, alone, with my arms outstretched and my lips puckered—waiting to accept that traditional, first-day-of-school good-bye hug and kiss. I went to her classroom to say good-bye. There she sat, at the table where her picture was taped, wearing a grin so big I thought her cheeks would explode. She sat straight and tall with her hands folded on the table—waiting. Let the learning commence!

That is how most Black children begin. They know something wonderful is about to happen and they bring with them an insatiable curiosity about the world around them, an unwavering focus on things that capture their interest, and an expectation that all the answers to their unlimited questions will be revealed—on the very first day! Just like most of us, Black children gravitate naturally toward interesting and intriguing activities and topics presented in ways that draw on natural learning instincts and preferences. So if all children are geniuses, you may be asking why this book focuses on the genius of Black children in particular.

It is our responsibility as educators to capture the interest of Black children and cultivate the natural genius they bring to our classrooms, but as our population continues to diversify, I often find that teachers are overwhelmed trying to incorporate the learning needs of so many children into the classroom experience. The challenge for many teachers is that the children in their classrooms represent many races, ethnicities, cultures, and languages—sometimes as many as fifteen different language groups in one classroom. In Seattle, children from the Horn of Africa alone (for example, Ethiopia, Somalia, Eritrea, and Djibouti) represent the second-largest group of dual-language learners in the public schools. Many teachers can't imagine what it would take to create a classroom that addresses the needs of such a diverse population. They commonly respond to the situation by saying, "I don't even know where to begin," and then stay with the teaching methods and strategies that are most familiar to them. Unfortunately, this means many children's learning needs and preferences will go unmet. When I'm coaching or mentoring teachers, I encourage them to address this challenge by starting with just one culture. Tackling fifteen cultures at once can seem daunting, but anyone can take on just one.

I started with just one culture—my own. (After all, most people know their own culture best.) I first examined research (both historical and contemporary) on Black learning styles and the cultural socialization that informs many Black children's expectations in their learning environments. I then began providing professional development and training on the learning needs and preferences of children of African descent to early childhood teachers whose classrooms consisted primarily of Black children. In 2011, I worked with several teachers over the course of one school year to transform their classrooms by increasing the teaching strategies, methods, and approaches they used to include more of the elements Black children might expect.

Including these elements is important because, just like my daughter, most Black children enter learning environments thinking of education as something that belongs to *them* and they see themselves as active participants in *their* education. For example, many children begin school trying to answer every question, touch every item, and share every experience. I think they are pretty sure the teacher's main job is to answer all their questions, hear everything the children have to say about the subject, and provide wonderful, exciting, interesting items to explore.

But by third grade, much of Black children's natural exuberance has been replaced by frustration and resignation. They begin to see education as belonging to the *teacher*, as what the teacher does in her or his classroom. Children develop this attitude when the teacher repeatedly stops them from talking and moving, limits what they can touch and examine, and requires them to be still and listen to the teacher talk. Many children become bored, and children who are bored and unengaged in school may look for something else to do. I see the same result when grown-ups are bored or unengaged in trainings. I see adults standing, pacing, tapping, knitting, talking, texting, and scrolling through screens on laptops, phones, and tablets. Grown-ups rarely get in trouble for such behavior, but children often do. When teachers have a stronger sense of what is needed by the learners in the room, they will be better equipped to engage those learners.

This leads to another reason I chose to focus on the learning needs of Black children in particular. Often, Black children who are bored and unengaged may behave in ways that are disruptive or may simply stop participating. The result is familiar: increased disciplinary action on the part of teachers, underachievement on the part of Black children, and low expectations on both sides. The worst-case scenario is when neither Black children nor teachers expect much of each other. Most people (children and grown-ups) will actively participate in a learning environment when learning is presented in ways that make sense to them, that make learning natural and fun, that make learning relevant. When Black children are allowed to do what they do best, to do what comes naturally, they become thriving, actively engaged participants in their own learning, and classroom management "challenges" that result from boredom disappear.

Increasing children's engagement is especially critical and timely as we look for ways to address the academic achievement gap and the opportunity/access gap that exists for many Black children. By implementing different learning styles and multiple intelligences in our classrooms and expanding our understanding of more personality types/traits, we can create learning environments in which Black children not only excel but also exceed our expectations. What if you could make what you teach more accessible to Black children? What if you could provide more opportunities for Black children to learn more? You can, and this book will tell you how.

I will begin by describing who I am talking about here. Who are "Black" children? Obviously, there are many ways to describe children of African descent: Black, African, African American, West Indian, South American, Latino, Afro-European, and so many more describing those who are biracial and multiracial. There are also wide variations among children of African descent *within* ethnic groups, based on a multitude of differences (economic, geographical, social, age, gender, political, and personality). For the purposes of this book I use the term *Black* to describe all children of African descent in the United States regardless of their individual ethnic backgrounds. In addition, I capitalize the pronouns "Black" and "White" because, in the case of race, we are talking about people, not colors—and I strongly believe that when a word designates a group of people that word should be capitalized.

▶ APPROACH

This book will present strategies for changing learning environments for Black children, strategies that incorporate more of the learning styles, multiple intelligences, and personality types/traits you learned about in education classes. You'll develop ways to combine and implement strategies we already know are effective so that Black children's learning needs are better met and supported. Black children are one of the largest populations in our early education and K–3 classrooms, and when we effectively support the learning potential of a group of children that large, we will have a significant impact in our profession and on Black children's futures. By gaining a broader understanding of what it looks like to expand your teaching potential in ways that are culturally relevant for one population of students, you will find it easier to move to another cultural or racial population of children and do the same. This approach doesn't narrow your teaching. It expands it to embrace *all* students and learning styles. This is doable! I will include familiar ideas and lots of concrete examples that aren't hard to implement. When you start small you will not be overwhelmed by the thought of creating the "ideal" learning environment.

▶ ORGANIZATION

This book is organized in two parts. Part 1 will provide you with background and context by answering the following questions:

- What, in general, do I need to *know* about learning styles, multiple intelligences, and personality types/traits?
- What is the relationship between *culture* and learning styles, multiple intelligences, and personality types/traits?
- What does the *research* tell us regarding learning styles, multiple intelligences, and personality types/traits in Black culture?
- Given the research, what tend to be Black children's *preferences* when it comes to teaching and learning?
- Where is the *disconnect* that seems to result in an academic achievement gap?
- How can I increase cultural *relevance* for Black children and eliminate the disconnect?
- What role does teacher *efficacy* play?

Part 2 will focus more on applied strategies and will answer a different set of questions:

- What are the *elements* of an appropriate learning environment for Black children?
- What *strategies* can I implement to expand my teaching?
- What can I do to make the classroom learning *environment* more engaging and relevant for Black children?
- How can I improve and strengthen my *relationships* with Black children, their families, and the Black community?
- How does this approach *look* in a classroom?
- How can I *incorporate* this approach into an existing model or curriculum?

When you finish this book, you will have a clear pathway for creating learning environments that support the learning styles and preferences of Black children and, in the process, increase access to more learning opportunities that will help all children, that will lift all boats. It's not a curriculum, but a way of thinking about how to implement a curriculum differently. It's about what you do and what it looks like.

▶ CAVEATS AND CONTROVERSIES

As I thought about this book, I was constantly reminded that a number of caveats and controversies need to be addressed up front and head-on.

Isn't good teaching good for everyone? Why would Black children need different teaching?

The more traditional perspective believes that good teaching is good teaching—that what good teachers learn and master works well for many (or most) students regardless of culture. Unfortunately, this belief could lead to an approach that says no one is different, that teachers can be successful with students from culturally, socially, and linguistically diverse backgrounds without having any special knowledge and skills beyond what they were taught in our teacher education programs. Of course, this line of thinking means that it's okay if you were not taught methods, strategies, and techniques for working with every one of the learning styles or multiple intelligences or for how to interact with different personality types/traits. Everyone should just try harder. Teachers should do more of what they already do, and children should try harder to learn from what they are presented.

But *should* both teachers and children just "try harder" and keep doing what hasn't really worked for either for a very long time? My perspective is that each child, just like each grown-up, is unique and learns differently. As grown-ups, we are better able to articulate our learning preferences and advocate for ourselves. If need be, we can even suggest (and expect to receive) changes in our learning environment to accommodate our needs, such as asking for a PowerPoint presentation to go with a training lecture. Children are less able to articulate their learning preferences, so we as teachers must recognize their needs. Good teaching is, indeed, good teaching; however, teaching that is most successful and most effective includes pedagogy and practices that address a variety of learning needs.

Does this lead to stereotyping or segregating Black children?

Stereotyping happens when we decide that one trait, preference, or characteristic applies to all members of a group. Segregation happens when we decide that those who learn differently cannot learn together. Yet those who oppose the perspective that there are learning styles based on race and culture have a valid concern. Many are concerned that identifying learning preferences based on race or culture will result in stereotyping Black children and may even lead to segregated classrooms. But by deciding that you *cannot* implement something because it applies to Black children is itself segregating or stereotyping. It would be like saying there *is* a way to teach Black children more effectively, but to do so would be singling them out. You are not stereotyping children by applying teaching strategies that let them use their preferred method of learning. And there is no need for segregation if you can effectively teach children who have different preferences. You won't have to single out or segregate if you expand your teaching repertoire by gradually incorporating into your classroom more elements of what you learned about learning styles, intelligences, and personality types/traits in your teacher education program. You will simply be increasing your ability to meet the learning needs of more children.

Is there really a Black learning style?

During the 1970s and '80s, a lot of research was conducted primarily by African American scholars who were concerned about the ability of most schools to meet the learning needs of Black children in the wake of desegregation. The bulk of this research centered on the cultural context of learning: researchers assumed that there is a body of knowledge, skills, processes, and experiences that is different from what is taught in most traditional teacher education programs; and that this knowledge is essential for preparing teachers to be successful with culturally and linguistically diverse student populations. Much of this research provided the impetus for the revision of the teacher education department at Pacific Oaks College Northwest in Seattle, where I served as campus dean for six years. Our focus was on providing our teacher interns with the knowledge base they needed to successfully educate children of color, English language learners, and children from low-income communities. We took what was a traditional teacher preparation program and added coursework regarding the cultural, social, linguistic, and political contexts of teaching and learning.

Indeed, when we look at early childhood learning environments around the world, we see a broad diversity in approaches to teaching and learning. It stands to reason that in a nation as diverse as the United States, a nation that grows more diverse each year, we will also find diverse learning preferences—including the learning preferences of Black children. Many Black children also learn in ways distinctly different from those of other cultural groups, which makes it imperative that our early childhood schools and programs expand their instructional approaches to accommodate these differences. We must remember, however, that not all Black children are alike. There will always be differences based on family income, country of origin, location (urban, rural, suburban), and parent education levels. Even highly individualized factors such as physical abilities must be taken into account just as they would be for any other population of children.

What about factors outside the learning environment? Couldn't those cause Black children's academic underachievement?

Some suggest that differences in academic achievement can be attributed to the social and economic challenges faced by many Black children and that it would be better to focus our attention on housing and nutrition. There is no doubt that circumstances *outside* school and work can have an effect on performance *inside* school and work. Remember, Maslow's hierarchy tells us that both children and grown-ups need regular, sustainable access to food and housing in order to focus adequately on school and work. And in the United States, approximately 26 percent of Black children are negatively affected by a lack of adequate food and housing (Iruka 2013).

Yes, food and housing challenges must be addressed, but not necessarily by classroom teachers. Classroom teachers have very little control or influence over children's home circumstances. They do, however, have control and influence over children's learning circumstances. Access to stable, high-quality, engaging learning environments is even more crucial for children in need. Circumstances outside the classroom can change for any child at any time, but circumstances inside the classroom can counteract negative factors by providing children with the excellent education they will need for their futures. Waiting for outside challenging factors to improve before attacking the achievement gap inside doesn't sound like a very promising academic plan for children in need.

▶ CONCLUSION

All of the perspectives noted here warrant keeping in mind. Not all Black children are the same, and stereotyping is rarely beneficial. Black children in large, urban cities will be different from those in suburban cities and those in rural areas. They will differ in socialization, assimilation, and academic preparation. On the other hand, cultural groups share "patterns of behaviors and interactions, cognitive constructs, and affective understanding that are learned through a process of socialization" (CARLA 2014). We must be careful to pay attention to group similarities *and* individual differences. I think there is too much "either/or" here. Who says that if we learn more about Black learning preferences, we have to create classrooms that are only for Black children? We currently limit learning preferences in our classrooms to a narrow range that meets the needs of a few, and we put *all* children in these classrooms. My approach would be to incorporate more learning preferences into *every* classroom.

Now that we have established some basic premises, let's move on to learning more about Black children.

PART 1

BACKGROUND AND CONTEXT

What does the research say regarding learning styles, multiple intelligences, personality traits, and their relationships to cultural influences in general and in Black children in particular? The next three chapters will provide more background and context to answer this question and take a look at the disconnect between what we know and what we do. Chapter 1 provides an overview of some programs and approaches that have been successful in educating Black children to high levels of academic achievement. The features and elements these learning environments share will serve as a backdrop for incorporating more culturally responsive learning preferences into classrooms (chapter 2) and for examining teacher efficacy and how teachers can increase their understanding of cultural influences on teaching and learning (chapter 3).

CHAPTER 1

What Do We Know about How Black Children Learn?

WHILE THERE IS QUITE A BIT OF RESEARCH outlining the learning preferences and patterns of Black children, we must keep in mind that not all Black children are the same, nor do they all have the same learning preferences and needs. Many Black children are comfortable with or have adapted to the more predominant strategies, methods, and approaches currently used. However, many Black children are not as successful in such environments. No one approach to teaching and learning works for everyone, be it a traditional, familiar approach or one that addresses the needs of specific populations of learners. In education, one "size" does not fit all, and the most successful and effective learning environments provide a broad range of approaches or "sizes," making it possible for more learners to find a good fit. For this reason, we must assist teachers in incorporating more learning styles, multiple intelligences, and personality types/traits into their classrooms; in chapter 2 I provide an overview of some of them. The more of these teachers can incorporate into their classrooms, the more learners they will accommodate.

▶ WHAT WORKS

Those who have studied the connection between culture and instructional approaches provide examples of classrooms and schools in which teachers have studied students' cultures and then revised curriculum or developed new curriculum more relevant to those cultures (Delpit 2006; Gay 2000; Ladson-Billings 1994).

Education has always been highly valued in Black communities, even during enslavement when simply learning to read was considered a crime punishable by death, beating, maiming, or, at the very least, being sold away from family. There has always been an internal, persistent drive to learn, to know more, which has resulted in the establishment of a remarkable system of Black schools and colleges. The Historically Black Colleges and Universities (HBCUs) in the United States have produced many of the Black legal, educational, scientific, and medical professionals in our country and continue to do so (Postsecondary National Policy Institute 2015; U.S. Department of Education 1991).

In addition to the HBCUs, numerous other schools and curriculum, historically and currently, have provided excellent educations for Black children. Several examples are outlined briefly in the following sections. I selected them because I heard and read good things about them and because a number of Black families selected these programs and schools for their children as alternatives to what else was available. All of them (according to their "self-reports," websites, books, and documentaries) have had positive results with Black children. Many of them share some common features that are compared at the end of this chapter and are related to the research discussed in chapter 2. Please bear in mind that these features are not exclusively successful with Black children. In fact, many children benefit from having these elements in their learning environments. However, you will see from the research presented in chapter 2 that these elements benefit many Black children as well.

HighScope

HighScope's mission is "to lift lives through education" while inspiring educators to inspire children.

The School and Population

HighScope began in 1962 as an experimental curriculum with 123 Black children at the Perry Preschool in a housing project in Ypsilanti, Michigan. The children were between the ages of three and four and attended the preschool for one or two years.

The Curriculum and Pedagogy

HighScope has a number of key features and elements:

Active Participatory Learning: Children have direct, hands-on experiences with people, objects, events, and ideas. They make choices, follow through on their own plans and decisions, and develop creative problem-solving ideas.

Plan-Do-Review: Children plan and make decisions about what they want to learn or work on during their Work Time. Then they are given ample time (at least thirty minutes) to put their plan into action, to actively engage in their own interests. At the end of Work Time, children review their plans, discuss how it went, and suggest changes for next time.

Key Developmental Indicators (KDI): HighScope has developed fifty-eight indicators based on eight curriculum content areas (approaches to learning, social/emotional development, physical development and health, language/literacy/communication, mathematics, creative arts, science and technology, and social studies). The KDIs are the basis of the HighScope assessment tool: the Child Observation Record (COR). To create the records, teachers take notes about children's behaviors, changes, and statements relative to each indicator to develop a fuller understanding of each child's development and progress.

Classroom Arrangement: HighScope classrooms encourage children to engage in meaningful personal and educational experiences. Numerous interest areas (including woodworking, computers, and outdoor areas) contain enough materials for multiple children to work at the same time and encourage choice.

Parent Involvement and Engagement: HighScope provides resources for parents (for example, Key Learning Experiences at Home—An Information Sheet for Parents) that explain how they can support the HighScope approach at home. In addition, home visits before school begins and multiple conferences during the year strengthen home/school ties. These activities allow parents, families, and teachers to work together as a team.

Problem Solving: Children are taught a six-step mediation/conflict resolution process that HighScope has designed for children as young as eighteen months old.

Adult-Child Interaction: Adults and children are partners in the learning environment, and shared control is central to their interactions. Teachers are responsive, guiding, and nurturing while also looking for opportunities to challenge children's learning and development.

The Results

The HighScope Educational Research Foundation has been tracking the original 123 participants for over forty years (HighScope Perry Preschool Longitudinal Study Project) and continues to find positive effects and influences over their lifetimes as a result of the practices, strategies, and approaches of the HighScope curriculum. According to *Lifetime Effects: The HighScope Perry Preschool Study through Age 40* (Schweinhart et al., 2005), Black children who participated at the Perry Preschool were more likely to exhibit the following characteristics:

- have higher IQs at age five
- be on target academically at eighth grade
- graduate from high school on time
- go to college
- earn higher wages
- be married and actively parenting their children (males and females)
- have medical insurance
- own a home

HighScope participants were less likely to have the following outcomes:

- be placed in a special education program
- receive social services such as welfare assistance and public housing
- be arrested for nonviolent crimes
- be arrested for violent, property, or drug crimes
- have challenges with substance abuse

In addition, the 2005 study included a cost effectiveness analysis indicating that for every $1.00 invested in high-quality early childhood education, society saves $16.14 in the cost of special education services, public assistance, unemployment, and dealing with crime. Research from the HighScope Perry Preschool Longitudinal Study Project has informed current educational preschool policy and planning, including the national plan of President Barack Obama's administration for expanding early education opportunities and the federal-state Preschool for All initiative.

HighScope's Perry Preschool Longitudinal Study Project is my favorite example of a research-based curriculum and an evidence-based school model. How HighScope's approach reflects some of the research regarding several learning preferences for Black children is presented in chapter 8.

Knowledge Is Power Program (KIPP)

The Knowledge Is Power Program (KIPP) is a nationwide network of free, lottery-based, open-enrollment college-preparatory schools in under-resourced communities throughout the United States. KIPP schools are usually established under state charter school laws, and KIPP is the nation's largest network of charter schools.

The School and Population

KIPP began in an inner-city Houston, Texas, public school in 1994 when founders Dave Levin and Mike Feinberg launched a program to help fifth graders gain the skills and knowledge to be successful in college and in their communities. The following year, Feinberg developed KIPP Academy Houston into a charter school, and Levin went on to establish KIPP Academy New York in the South Bronx. The original KIPP Academies have a sustained record of high student achievement.

According to KIPP's website, more than 95 percent of the schools' students are African American or Latino/Hispanic; more than 87 percent are eligible for the federally subsidized meal program. Students are accepted regardless of prior academic record, conduct, or socioeconomic background. However, KIPP schools typically have lower concentrations of special education and limited English proficiency (LEP) students than the public schools from which they draw.

The Curriculum and Pedagogy

The schools operate on the principle that there are no shortcuts to success: outstanding educators, more time in school, a rigorous preparatory curriculum, and a strong culture of achievement and support will help educationally underserved students develop the knowledge, skills, and character needed to succeed in top-quality high schools, colleges, and the competitive world beyond.

When a student is admitted to KIPP, a teacher or the principal sets up a home visit with the family and student to discuss the expectations of all students, teachers, and parents in KIPP. Students, parents or guardians, and teachers are all required to sign a KIPP contract agreeing to fulfill specific responsibilities, promising that they will do everything in their power to help the student succeed and go to college.

The program is organized to provide individual attention to students. The smaller, more intimate environment of the academy helps students feel more comfortable, and teachers keep better track of student progress. Interdisciplinary teams of two or more teachers work with the same group of students for a minimum of one year.

The Results

According to KIPP's 2014 "report card," 45 percent of KIPP alumni have earned a bachelor's degree and another 6 percent have earned an associate's degree, totaling over 50 percent earning a college degree. These results are from the early classes of students from the first two KIPP schools in New York and Houston. This is compared to approximately 22 percent of the general population of Black people eighteen and older in the United States who have a two-year or four-year degree and less than 1 percent who have advanced degrees (U.S. Census Bureau 2014).

Seattle Urban Academy

Seattle Urban Academy (SUA) is a small, independent school in Seattle, Washington, that began in 1989 as a small tutoring center. It is a division of CRISTA Ministries, a parachurch organization focused on education, world health, and human services.

The School and Population

SUA serves twenty-five to thirty-five low-income students of color in grades nine through twelve. Most of these students have not been successful in public schools and have been suspended or expelled, or have dropped out. The school prides itself on achieving success with students considered troubled or at-risk for academic failure.

SUA students must:

- be fourteen years or older;
- have experienced academic failure in previous schools;
- want to work through their personal challenges and take ownership of their academic, social, and spiritual growth; and
- want to graduate from high school and transition to higher education and sustained employment.

The Curriculum and Pedagogy

SUA creates a family environment by valuing each student's unique qualities. Students receive one-on-one academic support from teachers in addition to the individualized attention facilitated by small class size. This support provides students with the stability they need to graduate. Key elements include the following:

Spiritual Health: Teachers and staff are committed to helping students discover their identity, passion, and purpose so they can, in turn, contribute to the health of the greater community.

Academic Intensive Care and Mastery Standard: SUA is committed to helping students make up the one-to-seven-year gap in academic competencies that many of them face.

Social Growth and Maturity: Staff and students build relationships based on trust and deep caring to address the multiple risks in students' lives and provide resources that increase health and positive adult outcomes.

College Guidance: Because many SUA students are the first in their families to graduate to higher education, much focus is placed on helping students research and visit college campuses and completing admissions processes (college entrance exams, scholarship applications, and so on).

Career Development: To prepare students for employment, SUA provides career exploration, career fairs, job shadowing, and internship experiences based on students' skills, values, passions, and interests.

The Results

According to SUA's website, the school has had much success preparing its students for college and employment:

- 95 percent of SUA seniors graduate.
- 91 percent of SUA graduates go onto higher education or sustained employment.
- 65 percent of SUA students are employed (versus 25 percent of Washington State youth).
- 80 percent of SUA graduates who enter colleges or universities complete degrees (vs. 10 percent nationally for low-income students completing college degrees) (Calahan and Perna 2015; Executive Office of the President 2014).

These percentages are high, and the student population is currently around only thirty-two students; SUA's data are remarkable, however, considering that the students were on track to flunk out of public school.

Urban Prep Academy

Urban Prep Academies (also known as Urban Prep Charter Academy for Young Men or simply Urban Prep) is a nonprofit organization that operates three free, open-enrollment, all-male, college-preparatory, public charter high schools in Chicago.

The School and Population

The mission of Urban Prep is to provide a comprehensive, high-quality college prep education to young men that results in their success in college. Urban Prep was founded in 2002 by Tim King and a group of African American education, business, and civic leaders, and it received its first charter approval from Chicago Public Schools in 2005. It is the first all-male public charter high school in the United States.

Students are admitted to ninth grade through a lottery, with no evaluation of test scores or special needs. Some transfer students are admitted to grades ten through twelve. Approximately 85 percent of the students are low-income, and many are several grade levels behind in the core subject areas. Nearly all of them are African American.

The Curriculum and Pedagogy

Urban Prep structures its educational approach through four curricular and extracurricular "arcs":

The Academic Arc: a rigorous college prep curriculum that offers sustained attention to reading, writing, and public speaking skills

The Service Arc: a focus on deepening the students' sense of responsibility and identification of community needs by completing volunteer programs throughout the area

The Activity Arc: a focus on increasing students' confidence, interpersonal skills, and leadership qualities by participating in at least two school-sponsored activities per year, such as sports or clubs

The Professional/College Arc: an emphasis on providing students with valuable professional experience by requiring them to spend one day a week in a professional setting. This focus serves to reinforce character and leadership development in students, and provides them with work experience. The College Arc provides college enrichment programs during the summer at national and international colleges and universities.

Urban Prep promotes a positive school culture by emphasizing the "Four Rs":

- Respect: Students and staff members address each other by last names (Mr. King, Ms. Carroll) only.
- Responsibility: Students are held accountable to a strict code of conduct.
- Ritual: Students participate in daily, weekly, and yearly rituals such as Community and Tropaia to reinforce feelings of community and self-worth.
- Relationship: Urban Prep issues each staff member a cell phone whose number is distributed to all students so that students can have continuous contact.

Urban Prep has other unique features that are integral to its mission.

The Pride System: Each grade level at Urban Prep is divided into six groups of twenty students, known as "Prides" (named for the school's mascot, the lion). Prides (each consisting of students from multiple levels and abilities) function as smaller units within the school to provide each student with a mentor, as well as a peer-support network. Prides compete for points earned for good attendance and high grade point average, and through intramural athletic competitions. Prides may lose points for dress infractions, attendance violations, or other disciplinary infractions. The Pride with the most points is awarded the Pride Cup at the annual year-end ceremony, known as Tropaia.

Uniforms and Discipline: Urban Prep students must wear uniforms and follow a clearly communicated discipline program based on community and mutual respect. The school uniform consists of khaki pants, white buttoned-down and collared dress shirt, solid-red school necktie, and black two-button blazer with an embroidered school crest.

Summer Programs: During the summer, students participate in academic, professional, and service programs throughout Chicago and around the world, such as summer programs at the UK's Oxford and Cambridge universities, as well as elite stateside institutions including Northwestern University and Georgetown University. All incoming freshman must attend the summer program in August.

Athletics: Urban Prep campuses operate independent athletic programs that compete against one another and in the Chicago Public League.

The Results

Urban Prep's motto is "We Believe"—a constant reminder to all (teachers, administrators, staff, board of directors, community members, donors, and students) to reject negative stereotypes of and low expectations for Black males. From 2010 to 2014, 100 percent of Urban Prep's graduating seniors were admitted to four-year colleges or universities:

- 2010: 107 students admitted to 75 colleges
- 2011: 71 students admitted to 137 colleges (some accepted to more than one)
- 2012: 85 students admitted to 128 colleges (one was accepted to 14 different colleges/universities)
- 2013: 167 students admitted to 120 colleges
- 2014: 240 students admitted to 186 colleges

In 2006, the University of Chicago released a study reporting that only one-fifth of African American males in Chicago Public Schools would graduate from college (Roderick, Nagaoka, and Allensworth 2006). According to an Urban Prep April 8, 2014, press release posted on the school's website, "80 percent of Urban Prep's alumni are persisting in college."

Westside Preparatory School

In 1975, teacher and education activist Marva Collins created Westside Preparatory School, a low-cost private school, specifically for the purpose of teaching low-income African American children whom the Chicago public school system had labeled as being learning disabled.

The School and Population

"Working with students having the worst of backgrounds, those who were working far below grade level, and even those who had been labeled as 'unteachable,' Marva was able to overcome the obstacles" (Society of Saint Pius X 2014). Marva Collins believed a dedicated teacher would take the failure of even one child personally. She felt that complaining about how far behind a child was or what the child hadn't learned didn't help the child. After all, it was the teachers' job to catch children up and teach them what they didn't know. Westside Preparatory teachers were expected to respond to children with love and positive feedback and never engage in negative programming. After thirty-three years, the school closed in 2008 due to insufficient funding (Jordan 2008).

The Curriculum and Pedagogy

Westside Preparatory School (WPS) curriculum was based on the Socratic method with a focus on inquiry and discussion. Teachers and students ask and answer questions as a way to stimulate critical thinking and to present diverse and divergent ideas. The pace and the rate of information are managed by the teacher to encourage student participation and engagement, which reduces discipline issues. With the Socratic approach there is little place for worksheets and inane busywork. WPS established an intellectual atmosphere with the following elements:

- a general attitude suspending judgment in order to examine reasoning
- abstract content that has different meaning to different students in order to aid discussion and challenge students' logic

- teaching children to reason
- teaching, reviewing, and examining new words, called "the words to watch"
- a series of pertinent and thought-provoking questions as reading progresses
- predictions using logic, reasoning, and evidence
- teaching students to test their reasoning
- writing daily "letters" to authors or characters and writing critical reviews of works studied
- teaching children to refer to what they've learned to support their opinions

The Results

All WPS graduates entered colleges and universities, including Harvard, Yale, and Stanford. They became physicians, lawyers, engineers, and educators. "News of third grade students reading at ninth grade level, four-year-olds learning to read in only a few months, outstanding test scores, disappearance of behavioral problems, second-graders studying Shakespeare, and other incredible reports, astounded the public" (Society of Saint Pius X accessed 11 April 2014).

A Comparison of Programs

The accompanying table provides an overview of the curricular and pedagogical elements of the schools and programs discussed. I've included the Historically Black Colleges and Universities (HBCUs) because most were created at a time when African Americans were usually excluded from historically White colleges by law or prohibited from being educated at all.

CURRICULAR/ PEDAGOGICAL ELEMENT	BLACK COLLEGES AND UNIVERSITIES	HIGHSCOPE	KNOWLEDGE IS POWER PROGRAM (KIPP)	SEATTLE URBAN ACADEMY	URBAN PREP ACADEMY	WESTSIDE PREPARATORY SCHOOL
Close, authentic, meaningful relations with Black families and communities.	Teachers know they are educating the future Black community. Need to educate future Black professionals in a racially segregated society. Family and community involvement and engagement go both ways— teachers involved with Black families and community, who are both equally involved with teachers.	Resources to help parents understand child development and how it is fostered at school and home. Conducting home visits and multiple conferences with parents each year. Parents and teachers work together to promote children's learning.	Home visits with families. High expectations for families.	Service to the community.	Service to community and international service.	Desire to better serve Black families and children in the Chicago Public School system.
Working with students considered at-risk or behind and educating them to high levels.	Black students barred from White colleges by law or practice.	Began with low-income children from a housing project. Individual child observations based on curriculum goals.	A high percentage of educationally underserved African American students who are eligible for free/reduced-price lunch.	Students who have experienced academic failure and are considered "troubled" by previous schools.	Almost 100% African American males, high percentage low-income.	Low-income African American children considered learning disabled, unteachable, and coming from the worst backgrounds; children working far below grade level.

CURRICULAR/ PEDAGOGICAL ELEMENT	BLACK COLLEGES AND UNIVERSITIES	HIGHSCOPE	KNOWLEDGE IS POWER PROGRAM (KIPP)	SEATTLE URBAN ACADEMY	URBAN PREP ACADEMY	WESTSIDE PREPARATORY SCHOOL
A school and classroom sense of community, family, and belonging.	Small class size at many institutions. Strong alumni ties. Shared experiences of racism and discrimination.	Children learn to solve and resolve their social conflicts with each other in peaceful, respectful ways.	Small environments. Teachers have the same students for a year at minimum.	Small classes. Community "family" and environment where everyone belongs and is supported.	Multilevel and multiability "Prides" to create smaller units. Active participation in sports. Discipline based on community and mutual respect. Respect. Peer support.	Collins's promise to every single student that she would not let them fail—no dropping out allowed.
Commitment to teaching students who need support and a belief in the teacher's ability to do it.	Strong drive to educate African Americans. High teacher efficacy.	Belief that a child-centered curriculum based on the child's interests would increase academic achievement and future success.	No shortcuts to student success. High expectations for teachers. Culture of doing everything in your power for student success and understanding that you have a lot of power.	One-on-one personal attention. Academic "intensive care."	Teachers, staff, administrators, board of directors, community members, and donors believe in their students' potential.	Belief that teachers can catch children up and teach them what they don't know.

CURRICULAR/ PEDAGOGICAL ELEMENT	BLACK COLLEGES AND UNIVERSITIES	HIGHSCOPE	KNOWLEDGE IS POWER PROGRAM (KIPP)	SEATTLE URBAN ACADEMY	URBAN PREP ACADEMY	WESTSIDE PREPARATORY SCHOOL
High expectations for students and a rigorous, challenging curriculum.	Very high expectations for educating future professionals. Degrees cover a variety of content areas (professional, technical, and academic).	Adults assume children can solve problems creatively and master critical content in the process. Creative arts.	Rigorous curriculum. Culture of achievement and support. Preparation for quality schools and a competitive world. High expectations for students. Interdisciplinary teaching teams.	Expectation of content mastery.	Rigorous curriculum that prepares every student for college. Focus on reading, writing, and public speaking.	Challenging curriculum. Intellectual atmosphere. Introducing vocabulary, definitions, and meanings before engaging with content.
Holistic social and emotional development of students.	Understanding of students' cultural and social experiences.	Encourage conflict resolution and problem solving.	Intimate environments so students feel comfortable.	Focus on students' skills and passions. Integrating students' spiritual health. Focus on social development.	Character and leadership development. Rituals such as school crest and Pride Cup. Active participation in clubs.	Respond to children with love and positive feedback, not negative programming.
Strong, positive teacher-student relationships.	Shared control of classroom.	Strong teacher-child relationships and nurturing interactions.	Teachers promise to do everything in their power to help students succeed.	Relationships based on spiritual health and committed adults.	Every staff member is given a cell phone and the students are given those numbers.	Dedicated teachers take the failure of just one child personally.

CURRICULAR/ PEDAGOGICAL ELEMENT	BLACK COLLEGES AND UNIVERSITIES	HIGHSCOPE	KNOWLEDGE IS POWER PROGRAM (KIPP)	SEATTLE URBAN ACADEMY	URBAN PREP ACADEMY	WESTSIDE PREPARATORY SCHOOL
Students take responsibility for their learning.	African Americans' strong drive to be educated when faced with discrimination and exclusion.	Children take responsibility for their learning through Plan-Do-Review critique of their own work and their own learning.	Students promise to do everything in their power to succeed and go to college.	Students take ownership of their academic growth.	Students take responsibility for conduct and academic persistence.	
Students actively engage and participate in conversations, discussions, and learning.		Hands-on experiences with a wide variety of objects and materials that reflect children's interests. Active and participatory learning. Daily routine offers stimulating variety.		Career exploration aligned with students' values, passions, and interests.	Pride competitions for academic achievement.	Discussion and inquiry. Testing and examining students' logic and reasoning. Questions, evidence, and investigations. No worksheets and "busywork."

⏵ COMMONALITIES

All of these schools demonstrated the ability to successfully educate Black students to high levels of academic achievement. All of these schools also took into consideration the cultural and learning needs of the Black children they served. Some of the approaches and characteristics they demonstrated in common are as follows:

Start with the students, where they are right now. Almost all of these programs took on Black children whose academic needs were considered too challenging for traditional programs. Successful programs appear to build on each child's current strengths and use them to support new learning.

Give Black children who are behind more than a year of learning in the academic year. Children who are behind will stay behind if they are only offered one year of learning each year. To catch up in two years, they will need 1.5 years of learning each year to make up the difference. I'm talking about basic math facts. Any child who is behind will need more of what the other children are receiving if they are to catch up. In the schools I've discussed, bringing children up to grade level involved one-on-one teaching, academic intensives, high expectations, a belief in the student's ability to catch up, and probably some extended day/year options.

Focus on learning more than teaching. Children's learning was seen as the primary outcome of teaching in all of these programs. Yes, teaching is vital, but in successful programs, if learning isn't happening, teaching isn't happening.

Let children move! Many of the programs outlined here built in opportunities for movement through experiential learning, hands-on projects, experiments, creative arts, and sports.

Embed culturally relevant or Africentric curriculum, pedagogy, and engagement. Many of the programs embedded Black cultural perspectives and approaches into the curriculum by sharply increasing the amount of engagement they had with Black families and the Black community.

Learn more about Black history, Black culture, and the Black experience both in the United States and in Africa. Black people have a history and experience on earth that spans thousands and thousands of years. Successful programs did not limit their knowledge of Black people to the last four hundred years of their experience in the United States alone.

Let children talk! Let students use all the words, structures, mispronunciations, and creative grammar they have to offer in whatever language and/or dialect they use to offer them. Open-ended discussions between children and teachers and between children were common. Teachers weren't the only ones talking and did not appear to be talking most of the time. While children do need to become proficient in academic English, having a strong base of their home language to build on is probably a good place to start.

Let children solve problems. A review of all the curricula, teaching strategies, activities, and interactions showed many opportunities for Black children to debate, discuss, debunk, defend, figure out, work through, prove, and explain much of what they are learning.

Questioning is encouraged. A culture of inquiry and collaborative learning was prevalent. Teachers did not always have all of the answers, and there was much evidence of opportunities for teacher and children to explore topics and learn together.

Have high expectations. Teachers in these programs expected Black children to achieve at the highest levels, so they did. This was true even with children who were behind in key content areas and considered at risk of academic failure. In most cases, failure was never considered a viable option, good enough wasn't "good enough," and a D may have been a passing grade but it was not an acceptable grade.

Respect Black children, their families, and their communities. It was clear in most of these programs that the teachers respected the families and communities to which Black children belonged.

They did not see themselves as needing to "save" Black children from their families and communities.

Everyone thinks he or she can. These programs demonstrated a lot of efficacy. Teachers believed they could teach Black children effectively, so they did. Children believed they could learn from their teachers, so they did.

Here is what you do *not* find in the schools and curricula described:

- silent, still students and learning environments
- the extensive use of worksheets or other tasks requiring long "seat time"
- mind-numbing, inane busywork
- "objective" and impersonal relationships
- a preponderance of teacher talking—teaching as performance art
- the belief that Black children can't learn at high levels
- the belief that Black children's culture puts them at a disadvantage
- the belief that Black children's environment contains too many challenges for them to learn
- limiting the amount of contact with Black families to short teacher conferences
- a preponderance of focus on children's weaknesses
- making Black children feel that their language and culture are inferior
- "helping" Black children by lowering expectations for their achievement

▶ MOVING BEYOND

In this chapter, I have provided an overview of programs and schools that seem to work well for Black children and shared some of their commonalities. Unfortunately, there does not appear to be widespread use of these successful learning approaches with Black children on a more regular basis, particularly in large, urban school settings. For example,

HighScope practices are found to have lasting, positive effects for Black children who are considered at risk, but I am unable to find evidence of the widespread use of those practices with low-income Black children today, even though the U.S. Department of Justice's Office of Juvenile Justice and Delinquency Prevention listed HighScope as one of its programs that work to reduce bad behavior in youth (U.S. Department of Justice 2000).

It is time to bring it all into the light—and into your classrooms. In chapter 2, we will look more closely at the research on learning preferences, the influence of culture on those preferences, the influence of culture on the learning preferences of Black children specifically, and what happens when there is a disconnect between learning preferences and the learning environments we commonly see.

Incorporating Learning Styles and Preferences

As I stated earlier, learning styles and preferences represent the ways in which we like to take in new learning and have that learning sink into our long-term memory. There are as many different combinations of preferences as there are human beings, but there are commonalities as well—"preference buckets" where we find similarities. Many people, if necessary, can adapt to and make good use of most preferences, but learning preferences are like using your dominant hand— one hand just feels more natural and easier to use than the other. As teachers, we must develop a deeper understanding of children's learning preferences in order to create learning environments that are exciting, rich, dynamic, and interesting. This understanding encourages teachers to change their classrooms from ones in which children sit quietly and still at desks or tables, completing worksheets and listening to the teacher talk. Such an environment accommodates only a small portion of the learning preferences in the room. This is true for grown-ups as well as for children.

▶ THE VALUE OF INCORPORATING MULTIPLE LEARNING PREFERENCES

This chapter focuses on the "buckets" of learning styles, multiple intelligences, and personality types/traits that you are likely to find in your classrooms. All of them are valuable and equal. They are not hierarchical—some are not "better" than others. Unfortunately, it is quite easy to dismiss the learning styles, multiple intelligences, and personality types/traits of others as inferior or second class, not up to par with those we're used to seeing in traditional classrooms. We can minimize the importance of other learning preferences, but that doesn't make them less important or valid. Left-handedness may be less prominent or prevalent but it is *not* less important, less useful, or inferior.

We each do what comes naturally to us, that which requires little energy or thought. Part of the challenge for all of us is that it is not easy to understand how someone else would be comfortable doing something we can't. When I have to do something that is not natural or normal for me—like writing with my left hand—I forget that my uncomfortable experience is not universal. Of course, with a lot of practice, anyone could learn how to do what feels unnatural, but why would we make children work that hard to learn? Providing learning opportunities that address more learning preferences will give all children the chance to shine, to be the "star," and to demonstrate the wonderful things they can do. All the ponies on the merry-go-round are different, but they all get the chance to be at the front. Each child should have that same chance.

▶ OVERVIEW OF LEARNING STYLES, MULTIPLE INTELLIGENCES, AND PERSONALITY TYPES/TRAITS

Most teachers have been exposed to learning styles, multiple intelligences, and personality types/traits through their teacher education pre-service programs. Some of the information about common learning styles is based on works by David Kolb and Rita and Kenneth Dunn (Dunn and Dunn 1978; Kolb 1984). For multiple intelligences, many may be familiar with Howard Gardner's work (Gardner 1983) or perhaps the work of Thomas Armstrong (Armstrong 1994). And for personality type, many teachers are familiar with Myers-Briggs, but many psychologists prefer the Big Five trait models (Digman 1990). There are supporters, detractors, and critiques of all of the above, so there is plenty more to learn than what I will be sharing in this section.

Below is a brief overview of learning styles, multiple intelligences, and personality types/traits. Most teachers are familiar with many of the categories and descriptions, but many teachers may not have the depth of understanding of what each looks like when implemented in a classroom. The categories are presented in alphabetical order to offset the tendency to prioritize them based on what we usually expect to see in a classroom. I will briefly describe each one and then discuss how possible misinterpretation of learning styles might lead to inaccurate perceptions of student misbehavior. Following that, I will focus on the influence of culture in general and the research regarding Black culture in particular as it relates to learning preferences. Finally, I will present a compilation of those preferences that are shared by many Black learners.

Learning Styles

In general, learning styles represent the ways we prefer to take in and incorporate new information and have it "stick." Six of these styles are usually covered in most teacher preparation programs and are explained briefly as follows:

Auditory: "Listeners" learn best by hearing. This can mean listening to someone else or talking out loud (self-talk).

Experiential/Tactile: "Movers/Doers" learn best by touching and actively engaging with new information.

Interactive: "Talkers" learn best by discussing new information with others.

Observational: "Lookers" learn best by watching others do something first before engaging new learning themselves.

Reflective: "Processors" learn best by having time to think about what they've learned before fully incorporating it.

Visual: "Seers" learn best by having new information presented as words or images.

Most children (as do most adults) use all six learning styles to some degree, but each of us also tends to have one or two that we prefer over the others. Many classrooms emphasize Visual and Auditory learning with an emphasis on listening to the teacher and completing paper-based work while sitting still for extended periods of time. Think about your own preferences: What makes learning something new "stick" for you? Does it depend on what you are attempting to learn? Is there one style that doesn't work well for you at all? What do you do when faced with a learning situation where your least favorite learning style is being used?

My two preferred learning styles are Interactive and Visual. I love to discuss what I'm learning with others, and I often need a book or other print material to remember what I've learned or to refer back to if I forget. My least favorite is Auditory—what goes in one ear goes out the other. In any learning environment where there is a lot of lecture, I have learned to take extensive, almost verbatim, notes. Interestingly enough, however, I learn other languages best through a combination of Auditory and Visual learning. When I hear and read another language at the same time I pick it up so much faster than doing either alone. Like many people, I've learned to use different learning styles for different environments and subjects.

Multiple Intelligences

Interest in multiple intelligences has grown over the years and is often based on Howard Gardner's study of the many ways in which a person can be "smart." Although there is much debate as to the number of intelligences there are, eight of the most familiar ones can be described as follows:

Bodily/Kinesthetic (I know my body): Some people have intricate knowledge of how to move and use the body effectively. They intuitively understand the physics of how the body moves and works and can isolate muscles that most of us don't even know we have. They are dancers, surgeons, gymnasts, athletes, and others who have a heightened sense of body awareness. They communicate well through body language and like movement, making things, touching.

Interpersonal (I know you): People with Interpersonal intelligence have a gift for understanding and "reading" others. They enter conversations and groups easily and pay close attention to social cues and other nonverbal messages.

Intrapersonal (I know myself): Those who have strengths in this realm are usually highly reflective. They understand who they are, how they feel, and how they are likely to react in interactions with others.

Linguistic/Verbal (I know words): Those who have this intelligence are the "word expert" people. They tend to be strong readers, writers, and/or speakers. They enjoy "wordsmithing" and word-play, and may be very adept at learning multiple languages.

Logical/Mathematical (I know sequences and patterns): Many people mistakenly think that having this intelligence simply means being good at math, but it's more than that. People with this intelligence are also skilled in seeing and identifying patterns and sequences that most of us miss.

Musical/Rhythmic (I know notes, patterns, harmony, and beats): More than simply being good with a musical instrument or having a musical ear, those who possess this intelligence understand patterns, harmonies, and the "conversation" of music—how all the parts relate to, coordinate/contrast with, and play off each other.

Naturalist/Spiritualist (I know how I'm connected): This is one of the more recent intelligences proposed. People in this group are very much connected with nature and the natural world. This means understanding not only the earth's botanical, physical, and geological properties but also how humans are interconnected with our planet and the universe beyond.

Spatial/Visual (I know space and form): People with this intelligence have a gift for seeing how things fit and work together. They can "see" what a geometric shape drawn on a piece of paper would look like if it were folded into a three-dimensional object; they understand human flow and interaction in a given space. People with this intelligence can pack a truck so that the very last box fits in the very last space.

As you can see, there is much potential and opportunity for humans to excel in a variety of ways. And, again, we all have some level of skill and ability in most of these areas—we are just more highly skilled in one or two of them. However, in most of our current learning environments, the Linguistic/Verbal and Logical/Mathematical intelligences are overrepresented. Aspects of these intelligences, such as reading and math, are usually the ones measured by intelligence tests.

One way to determine your own multiple intelligences preferences is to answer two questions: What did you get into trouble for in school as a child, and what did you do in your free time? In school I got into trouble for two things: talking too much and reading. I was always chastised for "disturbing my neighbor" and frequently told "get your nose out of that book." On the other hand, guess what I did in my free time? Yes, I engaged others in conversations and I read books—usually the encyclopedia or the dictionary because no one took those away from me or made me put them down.

Personality Types/Traits

Personality has to do with individual differences among people in patterns of thinking, feeling, and behaving. I spend a little time on both the Myers-Briggs Type Indicator (MBTI) and the Big Five because there are strong supporters of both approaches. The MBTI takes four aspects of personality (attitude, information gathering, decision making, and approaches to life) and examines the two preferences within each one. The following provides a brief (very brief!) description of each of the four aspects.

> **Attitude—Introversion or Extroversion (I/E):** Do you prefer to focus on the outer world (Extroversion-E) or on your own inner world (Introversion-I)?

> **Information Gathering—Sensing or Intuition (S/N):** This describes how you like information presented and whether you prefer to focus on the basic information you take in (Sensing-S) or to interpret and add meaning to information (Intuition-N).

> **Decision Making—Thinking or Feeling (T/F):** When making decisions, do you prefer to first look at logic and consistency (Thinking-T) or at people and special circumstances (Feeling-F)?

> **Approaches to Life—Judging or Perceiving (J/P):** This is about structure when dealing with the outside world and whether you prefer to get things decided (Judging-J) or to stay open to new information and options (Perceiving-P).

The MBTI combines all of these aspects of personality (I/E, S/N, T/F, and J/P) to create sixteen general personality types/traits. It is far beyond the scope of this book to examine all sixteen, but much has been written about how these types are represented in the general population and within subpopulations (gender groups, cultural groups, occupational groups). Personality types have been studied on every continent, and all of the Myers-Briggs type preferences can be found in all of the cultures studied so far. While the distribution of types varies, there are also some similarities. For example, males in each culture tend to report a preference for Thinking more than females do (Myers et al., 1998). The Approach to Life found in typical learning environments tends to be Judging, which often involves rules, conformity, order, and schedules. Considering that many women (including those who go into elementary teaching) tend to prefer Judging over Perceiving (Kise and Russell 2004; Martin 1992; Rushton, Mariano, and Wallace 2012), it's not surprising this approach predominates in schools.

On the MBTI, my personality type tends to be ENFP. This means that I prefer to focus on the outer world, to interpret and add meaning to information, to first look at people and special circumstances, and to stay open to new information and options. This does not mean I'm like this all the time. While I'm definitely an extrovert energized by interactions with others, after a long day of teaching or training, I find I have no words left and have to go be "brain-dead" for a while. I'm also more Intuitive than not, but there are always situations where I find myself wanting concrete data when what I'm being told doesn't seem to match what I see happening. I am also well aware of my tendency to experience empathy (much more so than sympathy), but when there is too much inconsistency in a decision-making process, I may be the first to request a more logical approach. Finally, I am very much the Perceiving type, reserving the right to change my mind about something if presented with new information. However, when something drags on too long or when a tight deadline is looming, I may well just make a decision and move on to the next thing on the list.

As I mentioned earlier, although educators may be more familiar with Myers-Briggs, many psychologists prefer the Big Five personality traits. Each of these is on a continuum that covers two extremes and everything in between.

Openness to Experience (inventive/curious vs. consistent/cautious):
Are you the curious type who prefers unusual ideas, trying new
things, and having new experiences or adventures? Are you comfortable with subtlety, ambiguity, complexity, symbols, and abstrac-
tions? Or do you prefer more conventional, traditional, concrete
interests, and experiences that are more familiar? Are you more
comfortable with the straightforward, obvious, and plain?

Conscientiousness (efficient/organized vs. easygoing/careless):
If you score on one end of this continuum, you tend to like
plans, preparedness, discipline, order, and schedules. There is a
place for everything and everything is in its place. If you score
on the other end, you tend to be more spontaneous and impul-
sive and prefer taking advantage of immediate opportunities.
Everything is out and spread around so you can see where it is.

Extraversion (outgoing/energetic vs. solitary/reserved): Do you
prefer a breadth of activities that involve a lot of engagement
with the external world? Are you energized by social activities
and interacting with people? Or are you more low-key and delib-
erate, preferring depth in your activities? Are you less dependent
on the social world, preferring more time alone to reenergize?

Agreeableness (friendly/compassionate vs. analytical/detached):
If you are on one end of this continuum, you are very interested
in people's feelings, like to make people feel at ease, feel other
people's emotions, and are more trusting and generous. Or are
you on the other end, more skeptical about people's motives
and more cautious about other people's problems, feelings,
and needs?

Neuroticism (sensitive/nervous vs. secure/confident): Do you tend
to have a low tolerance for stress? Do you worry about things?
Is the glass definitely half empty? Or do you tend to be more
relaxed? Do you easily shake off negative emotions? Is the glass
definitely half full?

Keep in mind that the Big Five are on a continuum. This is not an either/or but more of a line with an infinite number of dots between one extreme and the other. In addition, someone could score high on one element of a factor (high on openness to new adventures) and low on another element of the same factor (not so open to trying new foods and tastes).

So, where do I fit in the Big Five?

Openness: I tend to be very curious and open to new ideas, experiences, variety, but as I get older, I feel less of a need to accomplish items lower on my "must do" list (hike 20 miles to a campsite with all my gear on my back).

Conscientiousness: Here it varies. My children would say I prefer plans, schedules, order, and preparedness. If you look in my office, you'll see stacks of books, piles of files and papers, everything spread out.

Extraversion: As with the MBTI, I am *definitely* energized by interacting with others and dependent on the social world.

Agreeableness: I am interested in other people's feelings and tend to be empathetic (as opposed to sympathetic), but that interest decreases as their interest in *my* feelings, comfort, and concerns decreases.

Neuroticism: I think I straddle the fence in Neuroticism. As a parent, I worry about my children, but I don't stress out about them. I express my emotions freely, but I don't see myself as emotional. As for the glass, it's not half empty or half full. It's the wrong size for the amount of liquid in it.

Reflections

- When you consider the nine aspects of personality outlined in the preceding discussion, where do you think you fit? You can always take one of the many tests available if you want a more accurate description of yourself, but it's a good idea to develop a self-awareness of your general tendencies and preferences.

▶ STUDENT BEHAVIOR

Most learning environments (for both children and grown-ups) emphasize only a few learning styles, multiple intelligences, and personality types/traits. By the time we become grown-ups, we don't have to accept and adjust to whatever learning environment is presented to us. We begin to demand and require that our individual learning needs be met. Children are not so fortunate. They get only the learning environment that is presented to them, and when it fits their learning preferences, they learn a lot. When it does not, children learn only a little and with great difficulty and expenditure of energy. Most of the time, they just get into trouble. You can expect to see children get into trouble for some of the following behaviors when the teaching preferences that are presented to them do not match their learning preferences:

- daydreaming
- doodling
- looking out the window and not at the teacher
- talking to self and others
- fidgeting and squirming
- getting up
- blurting out responses
- multitasking
- clashing with other personalities
- playing with language

- talking back
- touching the teacher's "stuff"
- trying to work with other students
- asking personal questions
- trying to show teacher/class what they can do
- "showing off"
- verbal jousting
- asking too many questions
- constantly missing homework deadlines

In most cases, when children engage in these behaviors, they get into trouble. Eventually, they may even be labeled as "bad" children who simply need more discipline and punishment. Here's another way to look at some of these children:

- The "daydreamer" may be a reflective learner who was processing the material presented.
- The "doodler" may simply be doing something tactile in order to concentrate.
- The child who was "looking out the window and not at the teacher" may be an auditory learner who actually *is* giving the teacher his full attention.
- The "fidgeter" who keeps squirming and getting up may well be longing for a chance to make use of her Bodily/Kinesthetic intelligence.
- The "verbal jouster" most likely is quite gifted in the area of Linguistic/Verbal intelligence and is simply taking the opportunity to play with his words.
- The child who is "constantly missing homework deadlines" may have a perceiving personality and just wants to stay open to more information and more options or may be less concerned about or focused on strict schedules for getting things done.
- The child who "talks to herself and others" sounds a lot like an extravert who needs to bounce her thoughts and ideas off the outside world around her.

Developing a fuller understanding of learning styles, multiple intelligences, and personality types/traits helps teachers see the behaviors of their students in a very different light. As one teacher put it, "What I thought were student deficiencies were a matter of my style. Often I can change something small in my classroom that makes a big difference in helping them be successful" (Kise and Russell 2004, 28). Just imagine how different a classroom looks and feels when teachers provide more outlets, activities, and processes that accommodate more children's natural preferences for learning. Just imagine being able to name something unique, special, and individual about every child you teach—something that can't be found in his or her file. Yes, you have to get to know every single child really well, and, yes, you have to do this every single year. However, if you begin incorporating more learning styles, multiple intelligences, and personality types/traits into your teaching, it will get easier every year to create an environment that serves and educates more children. Children show us every day who they are and how they like to learn. We just need to stop, look, and listen.

▶ THE INFLUENCE OF CULTURE ON LEARNING STYLES AND PREFERENCES

The field of cultural anthropology is a great place to find information about cultural groups and how they share similarities, tendencies, and preferences. In very basic terms, culture is the cumulative deposits of knowledge, values, practices, opinions, behaviors, and many other elements passed on from one generation to the next. It is both conscious (what table manners to use when company is present) and unconscious (how many times it's considered "normal" to blink in a given period of time). Culture influences so much of who we are that it is easy to forget that these influences vary from culture to culture.

Some of the elements of culture that influence learning preferences include patterns of communication, values prioritization, social interactions, relational patterns, performance styles, decision-making preferences, and strategies for resolving conflict. Many children enter our learning environments with the elements of culture that are familiar to them, that are similar to what they experience at home, but that may not be the culture of the learning environment. Knowing more about the cultural background of the children you will be teaching serves as the starting point for creating a learning environment that supports multiple opportunities for more children to do what they do and know best. It bears repeating that while there will be cultural similarities, there will also be individual differences. Care must be taken to avoid stereotyping children according to cultural groups and limiting their educational experiences. The goal is to expand your teaching methods and strategies, not replace the ones you currently use with different ones. There will also be children in your classrooms who will benefit from what you already do well.

▶ RESEARCH REGARDING AFRICAN AMERICAN CULTURE AND LEARNING PREFERENCES

In order to present a broad, general overview of Black children's learning preferences, I've read much of the research around ways people of African descent (both adults and children) approach the education process and the teaching/learning interaction. Many Black children come from a distinct, often not fully understood, culture that is deeply rooted in West African culture, traditions, values, and language. When starting school, however, Black children are expected to have already mastered European culture. In essence, many Black children may be entering a foreign learning environment and trying to adapt to a second culture (Berger 1988; Hilliard 1998; Wright 2012). Cultural socialization happens in every culture and in every family. My husband and I were from different ethnic backgrounds, but the dominant culture in our household was Black. Therefore, our children were socialized into Black culture.

What follows is an overview of the ways in which Black culture intersects with the learning styles, multiple intelligences, and personality types/traits previously discussed. You will notice that the research cited includes both older and recent information. I did this to show that, in most cases, what has been learned, studied, and researched has been around for some time, with multiple people indicating similar findings.

Bodily/Kinesthetic: One feature of African American culture is a rhythmic, movement-oriented approach to life that includes physical action and expression. This includes a heightened sense of body awareness and highly developed kinesthetic ability that is manifested though sports, dance, and intentional use of "body language." Often there is a dislike of extended periods of being still or sedentary or confining body movements to a small physical space. "Speaking" with hands, arms, and the rest of the body is very common (Berger 1988; Boykin 1983; Hale 2001; Hale-Benson 1986; Watkins 2002; Wright 2012).

Collaborative: African Americans tend to be collaborative and collective and prefer working together in groups. They often are synergetic learners who try to incorporate other people and personal relationships into all aspects of life. High value is placed on group effort toward a common or communal interest (Boykin 1983; Lee 2008; Shade 1986; Wright 2012).

Competitive: It may seem to contradict being collaborative, but African American culture also values competition. Competition involves challenging, testing, and pushing oneself to better performance. While this involves a level of independent action and self-sufficiency, competition pairs well with collaboration in the form of collaborative teams competing against each other, because many African Americans take a lot of pride in overcoming obstacles and barriers to success (Lee 2008; Willis 1989).

Creative Expression: Expressiveness can be found in almost every aspect of the African American cultural experience, and high value is placed on creativity, uniqueness, "flavor," and style. Individualism is encouraged in everything from music, dance, art, and sports to talking, walking, dressing, and feeling. Creative expression is a form of communicating thoughts, ideas, emotions, perspectives, and experiences. Jazz, an African American creation, is a perfect example. The mark of an expert is *not* being able to re-create music exactly as presented on a sheet of paper; it is being able to embroider and embellish the sheet music with your own unique, creative, stylistic flair. Creative expression is a considerable part of the African American approach to life (Boykin 1983; Boykin and Bailey 2000; Hilliard 1976, 1998; Shade 1986).

Experiential/Tactile: For African Americans closely associated with a high level of Bodily / Kinesthetic intelligence there is a tendency toward experiential and tactile learning—learning by experiencing, touching, doing, and personalizing. This also includes how time is perceived, especially social time, which is viewed in terms of the event rather than the clock (the party begins when everyone arrives, not "at 3:00"). A level of "body memory" is involved. Learning "sticks" because you did it, you manipulated it, or it was connected to an event. For African Americans, experiential learning also means past experiences are used to predict what to expect in future situations, which means entering brand-new environments and situations can require increased adaptability and flexibility (Boykin 1983; Boykin and Bailey 2000; Durodoyle and Hildreth 1995; Shade 1982; Willis 1989).

Harmony: There is an ancient Kemetic word, *ma'at*, that incorporates concepts of harmony, truth, balance, reciprocity, and justice. For African Americans, harmony means understanding how people, the environment, and the universe are interdependently connected. This also means integrating the parts of one's life into a harmonious whole and viewing things in their entirety, not in separate pieces (Boykin 1983; Boykin and Bailey 2000; Hilliard 1976, 1998; Shade 1986).

Interdependence/Communal: Family and community have a very broad meaning in African American culture, and many African Americans have a strong social orientation. There are strong kinship bonds, extended family networks, and connections to others in their ethnic group / community. This is true for past, present, and future connections, which results in a strong heritage and history identification and a high level of respect for elders (Boykin 1983; Boykin and Bailey 2000; Watkins 2002; Hilliard 1995b, 2002; Shade 1986).

Interdependence/Spirituality: African American concepts of communal interdependence and harmony come together to form another cultural aspect prevalent in Black communities—spirituality. Many have a strong belief that a power greater than humankind exists, and it is not uncommon to see visible ties to religious organizations in the Black community. This does not mean, however, that *all* African Americans are religious; being spiritual does not always mean being connected to an organized religion (Boykin 1983; Boykin and Bailey 2000; Hilliard 1995a; Shade 1986).

Interpersonal/Relationship-Based: Social interactions are a crucial part of the socialization and learning process for African Americans, and relationships are key in all interactions. African Americans tend to be very people-oriented and value people over objects. The Interactive learning style and Interpersonal intelligence may combine in a preference for learning in dialogue and conversation with those you know and who know you in return. "Knowing you" doesn't have to mean a longtime relationship, but it does mean taking time to recognize and understand individual difference and uniqueness. Being able to develop and appreciate authentic relationships with others is a primary step in creating a supportive environment (Boykin 1983; Durodoyle and Hildreth 1995; Hilliard 1995b; Kohl 1995; Shade 1986; Watkins 2002;).

Mental/Physical Challenge: The appreciation of a challenge is an aspect of competition discussed earlier. Discovery, endurance, problem solving, strength building, investigation, and reasoning are all part of the African American experience and address the appreciation for overcoming obstacles and barriers to success. There is a dedication to increasing mental skill and physical ability—to win the next chess game, to run faster, to solve the problem, to jump higher—to do better. Of course, this means that African Americans, like many other groups of people, have an aversion to tedious, mind-numbing, repetitive, unchallenging tasks. Such tasks are often met with resistance, reluctance, and, as a last resort, resignation. Practice and effort cannot be a futile, meaningless, fruitless series of exercises and tasks (Hilliard, 1976, 1989, 1992, 1998).

Realism: This aspect of African American culture combines elements of experiential, relationship-based, people-oriented, harmonious interactions. African Americans usually prefer authentic communication. They tend to have a straightforward, direct manner ("keeping it real") and pay attention to details. In keeping with their proclivity for reading body language, they will check to see if the emotion or intention they sense matches the words they hear. Pretend questions (asking a child if he wants blue or red pajamas when the objective is simply "go to bed") or questions you don't want answered (asking a child if she's ready for bed when she doesn't really have a choice) are not very common in African American interactions (Akbar 1976; Belgrave and Allison 2006; Wright 2012).

Social Environment: Closely related to realism is attention to and reliance on information from the social environment. African American culture tends to be field dependent and highly contextual—a lot of meaning, communication, and understanding comes from nonverbal cues such as gestures and expressions. Meaning is verified by what is seen more often than by what is heard. This begins almost from birth in social gatherings as babies are passed from person to person, lap to lap, developing their own emotional expressiveness and becoming responsive to what others feel and think, to the emotional cues of others. African Americans tend to have a high degree of integration of feelings with cognitive elements and in social interactions may focus more on the people in the situation than on the tasks (Berger 1988; Curenton 2004, 2011; Hilliard 1998, 2002; Wright 2012).

Verbal: The use of language, playing with language, and linguistic challenges are easily found, appreciated, encouraged, and cultivated in African American culture and are based on African oral traditions. Again, it's not what you say, but how you say it. High value is placed on charismatic, stylistic use of language in very expressive ways. It is found in ministry and churches, rap and hip-hop music, and ritualistic word games and verbal jousting.

Richness of imagery in informal and formal language through the use of metaphor, hyperbole, and inference can be found in the show-and-tell stories of a four-year-old all the way to the inaugural speech of a president (Belgrave and Allison 2009; Berger 1988; Boykin 1983; Curenton 2011; Curenton and Iruka 2013; Curenton and Justice 2004).

Verve/Stimulus Variety: African Americans tend to live lives filled with a multilayered, energetic level of spirit and enthusiasm. There is a tendency to prefer an active, synergetic environment filled with simultaneous talk and multiple activities, so one is attuned to several stimuli rather than a quiet, routine, or bland environment. Conversation, music, children running around, and chess games all occurring at the same time are not uncommon at African American gatherings. Animated expressiveness—vivacity—is often the goal (Belgrave and Allison 2009; Boykin 1983; Hilliard, 1998; Shade, 1982, 1986).

▶ LEARNING STYLES AND LEARNING PREFERENCES OF CHILDREN OF AFRICAN DESCENT

Earlier I gave an overview of the research regarding learning styles, multiple intelligences, and personality types/traits. The following is a more condensed list of the tendencies that appear to show up most often in Black children, followed by a fuller explanation of what that means in a classroom setting. Each tendency is a combination of styles, intelligences, and personality types/traits.

- Bodily/Kinesthetic—learning through moving, doing, engaging, and touching
- Collaboration—working collectively, small-group work
- Competitive—challenging, testing, pushing oneself to better performance
- Creative Expression—singing, dancing, rapping, playing instruments, drawing, sculpture, drama, writing
- Experiential/Tactile—learning through engaging, manipulating, touching, personalizing, and humanizing

- Harmony—being a person and living a life that is balanced, interdependent, integrated, and connected
- Interdependence/Communal—being connected to family and community in the past, present, and future
- Interdependence/Spirituality—having a sense of a higher power, being connected to nature, to something bigger than oneself
- Interpersonal/Relationship-Based—knowing you and your family, caring about you, seeing you in other contexts, interacting with others, making a personal connection
- Mental/Physical Challenge—using critical analysis, critiquing, asking authentic "why" questions, using your body in dance, sports, drama, sign language, having an appreciation for overcoming obstacles and barriers to success
- Realism—not tolerating rhetorical questions, questions you know the answer to, or pretend questions; having authentic relationships; not tolerating "hidden" rules or anything abstracted into nonexistence
- Social Environment/Visual—learning through seeing, observing, experiencing, and feeling others; "reading" people's body language, facial expressions, emotions
- Verbal—using expressive language; playing with language, discussion, metaphor, hyperbole
- Verve/Stimulus Variety—engaging in multiple activities and stimuli in an energetic, exciting, expressive environment

Bodily/Kinesthetic/Experiential/Tactile

This may be an area that teachers find more challenging to implement because it is not at all like a "typical" learning environment. It can be a bit noisy with a heightened level of activity. It runs contrary to the notion that "schools were created by girls for girls." Many female teachers, myself included, have memories of "playing teacher" when we were girls. You gathered your dolls and stuffed animals and lined them up in neat rows. Then you proceeded to "teach" them by writing stuff on blackboards or sheets of paper. It was so much fun—and so orderly! Your "class" never moved, interrupted, spoke out of turn, or misbehaved in any way. Then one day another student (perhaps a little brother) came to join the class. He moved around a lot, asked questions unrelated to what you were doing in the front of the room, knocked over the dolls and stuffed animals, and was resistant to your instructions to sit still and be quiet. So he was sent to the "principal's office" (Mom).

These learners prefer a learning environment that is filled with movement, active engagement with materials, and time to spend touching and handling items in their classrooms. When these learners have to sit too long listening to talking or doing paper-based work at their desks, they become antsy and fidgety and may lose mental focus because the content is too abstract, too disconnected from their personal experiences.

> I read stories to my children every night when they were young. When Aaron was about three and a half, he started getting up while I was reading and going to the other side of the bedroom to play with his toys.
>
> Me: Sweetheart, I'm not finished with the story. Come back over here, please.
>
> Aaron: That's okay, Mom. Just keep reading. I can hear you. I don't need to see you to hear you.

Collaboration

Although collaboration and small-group work are talked about a lot as we look at our early childhood classrooms, I find that teachers have some difficulty implementing these approaches if they are feeling the pressure to conduct lots of individual assessments of children's learning. Collaborative learners accommodate and integrate content better if they are working with a team or group. In such situations, not everyone is doing the same thing or is achieving at the same level, and this allows for a lot of peer teaching and learning. Children learn so much more from each other than many teachers realize or appreciate. Children explain things to each other in their own language, not the teacher's language, and provide each other with real-life experiences and examples that help the content "make sense."

In many cultures, there is an expectation that important work and achieving goals is done collaboratively. Few would find a lot of value in attempting to "save the world" all by themselves. This is generally not the case in U.S. culture, where we are all expected to pursue individual achievement, pull ourselves up by our own bootstraps, and compete individually to be the one "winner." What's perplexing, of course, is that in the workplace there is an increasing demand for teams and teamwork. There is an African saying that if you want to go fast, go alone. But if you want to go far, go together. It stands to reason that many Black children may prefer collaborative learning environments.

Creative Expression

Creativity is what allows us to express ourselves in unique ways. It is an outlet for feelings, thoughts, ideas, frustrations, joys, politics; it's a way of "saying" something about ourselves as individuals. Learners who seek creative expression thrive in learning environments that are not constrained by the limitations of cookie-cutter, rote responses (which are not the same as "call-and-response"), copying off the board, filling in the blanks, connecting numbered dots in a classroom where everyone does the same thing, in the same way, at the same time. Creative expression requires permission to embellish, to elaborate, to "decorate" one's work and set it apart from the work of others, and many cultures place a high priority and significant value on creative expression in areas such as oratory, music, storytelling, and dance.

In a classroom, the learning task provided by the teacher (a picture to color, an item to draw, a phrase to copy, or a song to sing) serves as a template, a starting point, not the end product. The goal is to take what is presented and make it different, special, unique. Such creative learners often color outside the lines, add more details to the drawing, invent new verses for the song. An adult example can be found in some of the early jazz artists who let the other musicians replicate what was on the sheet music while they improvised, embellished, with music of their own invention—music that could not be reproduced by someone else. Unfortunately, many of our learning environments limit such individual expression or eliminate opportunities for creative expression when budgets are strained or restricted.

Harmony/Interdependence/Spirituality

This aspect of a learning environment can be confusing and misunderstood as teachers face the challenge of trying to distinguish between harmony, community, spirituality, nature, and religion. In some cultures, these are all the same concept, but in others they are different. In the context of spirituality and nature, learners with these intelligences feel a strong connection to "something bigger" than themselves. They are of the earth, not just on it. They are individuals but know that they are irreversibly and eternally connected to all of humankind—past, present, and future. They are part of a family and community with a shared experience, both current and historical. All of existence is interdependent on a biological, chemical, social-emotional level. We are not just human beings. We are humans being. There is a need for harmonious existence and interaction—a balance between each person and everyone and everything else.

So what does this concept mean in a classroom full of three-year-olds? Children with this learning preference need opportunities to contribute to the well-being of the plant world, the animal world, and the human world. Taking care of something living—be it the avocado seed, the gerbil, or the elderly lady across the street—combines opportunities for children to "locate" themselves in their families, their communities, and the natural world with opportunities for increasing healthy social-emotional development. Outdoor experiences and connection with nature are growing in popularity in many classrooms, but there are many more classrooms where children are not given these opportunities. This may be due to the challenge of figuring out how to connect with nature in highly urbanized environments or the challenge of finding time for service projects in high-stakes testing environments. Finding connections to nature in students' family and community environments will build on and strengthen Black children's sense of communal interdependence.

Interpersonal/Relationship-Based

Those with Interpersonal intelligence and those from Relationship-based cultures are constantly trying to get to know the other person with whom they are interacting. These learners will want to know everything about you and will want you to know everything about them. "Getting to know you" is important in establishing the underlying foundation of the teaching/learning interaction. Many of the Interpersonal/Relationship-based learners can't learn as much from strangers as they can from someone they know and who knows them. Teachers with these learners in their classrooms tell of their children wanting to know if they have pets or boyfriends, where they live, whether they go to church, if they have kids, what they like to eat, and countless other questions that help children learn more about the person who is teaching them.

Another aspect of teaching Interpersonal/Relationship-based learners is that there are many contexts within which a relationship is formed. These learners want to see you in other contexts and they want you to see them in other contexts as well. For many children this is what distinguishes a "talking head" from "my teacher." When you run into your students in the grocery store, when you attend their weekend sports events, when they see you in the audience at their performances, or pass by you in the park—these are the experiences that help children establish the kind of relationship with teachers that greatly enhance the teaching and learning in the classroom.

Mental/Physical Challenge

Most children love a mental challenge—especially young children. They are often on the "hunt" for something new to experience. They are natural scientists, explorers, inventors, creators. There is much research discussing the need for young children to have many stimulating experiences in order to take advantage of early brain development. A muscle that is not used or stimulated atrophies, dies. And yet, so many children are deprived of access to such stimulating and mentally challenging learning environments. Most children need, want, and long for opportunities to analyze, critique, study, and ponder. They want to figure things out, make hypotheses about what will happen, and have full and authentic answers to their "why" questions.

Learners who are not given adequate mental challenges are the ones most likely to act out or engage in classroom behaviors that are not conducive to learning. Children become frustrated and, perhaps, angry when they are bored and not allowed access to anything that challenges their brains to do more, think more, find out more. By the fourth grade I had come to the conclusion that teachers did not want you to read, and by seventh grade I had come to the conclusion that they did not want you to *know*, they just wanted you to *recite*. Children's learning environments need to have spaces and time and materials that allow them to follow their own interests and seek answers to their own questions. And it does not require financial resources to ask children stimulating, problem-solving questions that make them ponder, think, figure out, and reflect; simple language and plots bore most children.

Very much related to Bodily / Kinesthetic / Experiential / Tactile learners, children who love a physical challenge (many of them boys) need opportunities to push themselves physically to see what they can do, to use their Competitive tendencies. Little boys are often competing with their classmates trying to jump higher, run faster, and throw farther than anyone else. Unfortunately, in too many of our learning environments, the time allotted for physical activity is decreasing, even when we try to add more outdoor time. And although Collaboration is discussed separately, it is important to remember that competition and collaboration can work quite well together. Having teams that compete against each other, where there is collaboration within the team and competition between the teams, is a good example. But in trying to increase collaboration, teachers may have gone too far in one direction and restricted competition, with the result of limiting both boys' and girls' opportunities to develop their Bodily / Kinesthetic intelligence. Physical challenge doesn't always have to involve competitive sports, however. Incorporating dance, drama, and even sign language into the learning environment will provide more opportunities for more children.

Realism

This is closely related to the preference for relationship-based teaching and learning interactions. With realism, there is a need for a real relationship that can only be established over time. Rhetorical questions are quite common in U.S. culture. We ask people how they are doing and may be annoyed if they actually begin to tell us. We ask about their weekends and hope they say "great!" so we can move on. For many learners, rhetorical questions are a waste of time. If you don't want to know what that little girl did over the weekend, please don't ask her. She will go into great detail regarding everything that happened from the moment she left school on Friday. If your question really was rhetorical, she will not realize that the "polite" answer would consist of only one or two words. She will think you do not care about her weekend and, by extension, may not care about her.

Realism is imbedded in the learning preferences of young children who are still concrete learners, so you must also pay attention to how many times you ask children questions to which you already know the answer. This does not apply to testing children or assessing their learning. This refers more to questions with obvious (to the child anyway) answers such as, "Why did you take his toy from him?" Every child knows that you take a toy if you want to play with the toy. A more realistic response would be to acknowledge that he wants the other child's toy and then discuss better solutions. This is also the case with "pretend" questions. Too often, usually in an attempt to be polite or kind, we ask a question when we should have made a statement.

> TEACHER: Are you ready to take a nap?
> CHILD: No, I don't want to take a nap.
> TEACHER: Well, you have to take a nap because it's naptime.
> CHILD *(to him- or herself)*: Then why did you ask me if I
>   wanted to take one if I have to?

Social Environment/Visual

Visual learners actually have a collection of several different visual preferences—people, words, and/or pictures. They learn best by seeing. Visual-People learners tend to be quite observant when it comes to "reading" people, paying close attention to the body language, facial expressions, and tones of voice of others. When observing someone, they often make comparisons between what the person is saying, their tone of voice, their facial expression, and their body language. If they aren't congruent, or do not match, these children may become confused or suspicious and may even ask clarifying questions to see what's wrong. For example, no matter how much the brand-new, freshly minted teacher smiles on that first day of school, the Visual-People children will be trying to determine if the teacher is feeling nervous, excited, insecure, or passionate, and if the facial expressions, tone of voice, and body language match what they are sensing. This can be a little disconcerting for the teacher, so it's good to remember that such a skill is a sign of healthy social-emotional development.

Visual-Picture and Visual-Word learners like to see a visual representation of the information presented. This does not necessarily mean lots of picture books. Visual-Picture learners like charts and graphs and mind-maps that show them, at a glance, the concept or information being taught. Visual-Word learners prefer to read the information. Most of us need a balance between print and picture. When I'm reading research with a lot of heavy data, I may find myself getting lost in all the words, percentages, and formulas. With a chart or graph I can internalize the relationship between all those things in an instant. On the other hand, while a picture may be worth a thousand words, there are times when I really need the thousand words to provide me with more descriptive information than what is represented in a picture.

Verbal

It goes without saying that Verbal learners love words. I know because I'm one of them. Verbal learners have a multitude of skills and abilities and many of them are represented in typical classroom settings, but some are not. Most teachers are familiar with the strong readers, children with extensive vocabularies, and those most adept at using standard/academic English. Verbal learners also have many other talents. Many really enjoy wordplay, imaginary language, talking with others, and engaging in expressive language full of analogy and exaggeration.

I was frequently in trouble in school due to my desire to play with, manipulate, and create language. In the fifth grade we were learning about conjunctions—those words that connect parts of sentences. When I was asked to name one, I selected *but*, and when my teacher asked why it was a conjunction I said because it connects our back with our legs. I was sent to the principal's office. When I was learning French in seventh grade, our teacher asked some rote questions to which we were to respond with rote answers:

TEACHER: Où est la plume? (Where is the pen?)
STUDENT: La plume est sur la table. (The pen is on the table.)

This pattern went on for a while. Then came my turn.

TEACHER: Où est le livre? (Where is the book?)
ME: Je pense que le livre est sur la table, mais je ne sais pas parce que . . . (I think the book is on the table, but I don't know because . . .)
TEACHER: Non!! Le livre . . . est sur . . . la table! (No!! The book . . . is on . . . the table!)
ME: Bon! Le livre . . . est sur . . . la table! (Good! The book . . . is on . . . the table!)

I repeated my teacher's sentence in the same rote, staccato voice she used, but without her accompanying hand clapping. I was sent to the principal's office. Some of my teachers thought I had a "smart mouth" and maybe I did, but I still think they should have had more appreciation for my verbal and linguistic skill and ability. I just wanted to play with language and see if I really understood it or if I was merely parroting and reciting a teacher's words and random bits of information.

▶ SO WHERE'S THE DISCONNECT?

Earlier I talked about learning preferences in terms of using your dominant hand and how being right-handed isn't better than being left-handed. It's just different. The disconnect between learning preferences and the learning environment happens when you get into trouble for being left-handed. My mother was left-handed. When she was growing up in the 1930s and '40s it was common practice to force left-handed children to use their right hands to write. It didn't matter that she wasn't good at it, and it *did* mean that her penmanship was considered atrocious because she was still required to perform at the same level as her right-handed classmates. Much of the same set of circumstances pertain to Black children in their learning environments because, unfortunately, much of what happens in our learning environments is exactly the opposite of what Black children need to learn effectively and efficiently. When children are in learning environments that don't meet their needs, the usual result is the boredom and frustration that inevitably lead to misbehavior, underachievement, and possible placement in special education.

I also believe that some of the disconnect happens because too many teachers and researchers focus on what's "wrong" with African American children, what's not working well in their lives. This leads to pathologizing Black children, when what they need is improved pedagogy. Black children need to be taught, not studied. They need us to spend more time on what's "right" and on implementing what works or what has been recommended in all the research and studies that have been conducted for years. On the next page is a table adapted from Dr. Asa Hilliard's 1992 work about what many typical learning environments are like and what Black children may prefer (374).

From kindergarten through eighth grade my children attended a Catholic school that was predominantly African American and mixed-race. The school went to great efforts to really understand the learning needs of its students, and much of what was found in the learning environment there matched what Dr. Hilliard describes in the right column. In ninth grade two of them went on to Catholic high schools and one, Aaron, decided to attend public school. After a month of school Aaron came home frustrated. He said he didn't like his new school because it was a waste of his time. He said he felt like he was spending all of his time doing his teacher's work for her. "She gives us worksheets and we fill in the blanks for her. She writes stuff on the board and we copy it down for her. She makes us read our textbooks out loud for her. And when we're not doing that she makes us sit and watch her 'act' in the front of the classroom. I can't do this every day." And he didn't. He ended up changing schools, but not before things got worse.

When teaching and learning preferences collide, the child is usually the most injured. Children's reactions to this disconnect can range from inattentiveness to open resistance and an emotionally defensive posture as they attempt to "protect" themselves from a learning environment that conflicts with normal levels of activity, exuberance, and active engagement with the materials, items, and projects in the room. And as Black children move through their educational experience, more and more of what they need is eliminated—art, discourse, music, debate,

TYPICAL LEARNING ENVIRONMENTS	WHAT THE LEARNING ENVIRONMENT COULD BE
Analytical	Relational
Rule-driven	Freedom-loving
Standardized	Variation-accepting
Conformist	Creative
Memory recall of specific facts	Memory recall of essential ideas
Regularity	Novelty
Rigidity, order	Flexibility
"Normality"	Uniqueness
Difference = Deficit	Sameness = Oppression
Preconceive	Improvise
Precision	Approximation
Logical	Psychological
Atomistic	Global
Egocentric	Sociocentric
Convergent	Divergent
Controlled	Expressive
Meanings are universal	Meanings are contextual
Direct	Indirect
Cognitive	Affective
Linear	Patterned
Mechanical	Humanistic
Individualistic	Individual within group
Hierarchical	Democratic
Isolation	Integration
Deductive	Inductive
Scheduled	Targets of opportunity
Thing-focused	People-focused
Constant	Evolving
Sign-oriented	Meaning-oriented
Duty	Loyalty
Docility expected	Assertiveness accepted
Identification with African heritage is shamed	Identification with African heritage is intentional

drama, recess, group work, communalism, social interactions, stimulus variety—all disappear as the years go by. Learning becomes increasingly inaccessible and unattainable and Black children fall further and further behind. And most don't even know why!

The good news (yes, there is good news) is that this situation is all about to change for you and your students because you are taking the first steps toward increasing learning opportunities and access to education by incorporating more learning styles, multiple intelligences, and personality types/traits into your learning environments.

CHAPTER 3

Cultural Intelligence and Teacher Efficacy

In CHAPTER 2, WE EXAMINED THE INFLUENCE of culture on learning styles, multiple intelligences, and personality types/traits in general and the intersection with Black culture in particular. In this chapter, we will take a closer look at the importance of culture, cultural competency, cultural relevancy, and efficacy in the teaching and learning process. Our culture tells us how to think and what to think about, what to judge and how to judge it, how to act and how not to act, what is good, what is bad, what is right, what is wrong, what is appropriate, and what is unacceptable. Since culture embraces us, we should embrace it—in all of its presentations and manifestations.

▶ CULTURE IN THE TEACHING AND LEARNING PROCESS

In our classrooms, each of us (teachers and children) looks to our culture to provide clues regarding what should be taught, what should be learned, and how both of these efforts are supposed to take place. The teaching and learning environment we are most competent in is the one we don't have to think about, the one where teaching and learning expectations and practices align with our cultural expectations and practices. This is how we experience *cultural relevancy*. When something is culturally relevant, it fits; it makes sense. We don't have to spend a lot of time and energy figuring out the "whys" and the "wherefores" because we can make assumptions about what should be or what is supposed to be and just do what seems to be most natural. This is how we demonstrate *cultural competency*. Everyone has a culture and everyone is competent in at least one culture. Most of us belong to several cultures (gender culture, religious culture, regional culture, age culture). When you are immersed in your own culture, you feel like an air breather—everything comes naturally to you and you don't need to think a lot about your culture. But if you find yourself in a culture that is different from yours, you may feel like you are underwater and you realize rapidly that you are an air breather, not a water breather. Gaining competency in a culture takes time, years in fact, and it involves ongoing, continuous learning and growth that begins at birth. I have had fifty-nine years (so far) of being an English-speaking Black female in the United States, and I am continually learning more and more about what that means, what it means to and for me, and what it means to and for those whose lives I touch. In other words, gaining competency at anything in general and life in particular should be an ongoing process. We should never be done.

Cross-cultural competency is the ability to adapt effectively in cross-cultural situations and interactions (racial, ethnic, cultural, linguistic, economic, religious). With high levels of cross-cultural competency, an effective teacher of any cultural background can draw on Black children's culture to provide the appropriate scaffolding between where an individual is currently functioning, where she needs to be tomorrow, and what she needs in order to master more advanced skills and concepts. Teachers with high levels of cross-cultural competency usually have high levels of confidence in their ability to recognize cultural influences and use them in the teaching and learning process. Those with low levels of cross-cultural competency usually have low levels of confidence in their ability to teach effectively in a culturally diverse environment because they don't know what to do. This may be why so many Black children are labeled as problems or as having "special needs" both by teachers who are unfamiliar with Black culture in general and those who are unfamiliar with how to incorporate it into their classrooms (Lazara et al. 2009; U.S. Department of Education 2010).

▶ CULTURAL INTELLIGENCE

How do you go about increasing your cross-cultural competency? One way is by increasing your Cultural Intelligence. In chapter 2, I provided an overview of eight areas of intelligence that many teachers learn about in their teacher preparation programs. Cultural Intelligence is the "new kid" on the multiple intelligences block (Gelfand, Imai, and

Fehr 2008, 376). The term *cultural intelligence* (CQ) was developed as a research-based way of measuring and predicting an individual's intercultural performance (Earley and Ang 2003; Ang and Van Dyne 2008). In general, it is the ability to relate, work, function, and manage effectively across cultures and in culturally diverse settings. Having a high level of cultural intelligence can help teachers overcome many of the cross-cultural challenges they encounter in their classrooms. Based on the research of Ang and Van Dyne, there are four aspects of cultural intelligence:

Awareness: Knowing that there are differences and similarities between all cultures and respecting other cultures by questioning your assumptions about other people.

Knowledge: Acquiring knowledge about your own cultural preferences, practices, norms, and conventions and those of others through education and personal experiences.

Energy: Investing and directing time and effort into learning about the strengths and preferences of other cultures with the expectation that you can function successfully in those cultures.

Actions: Having a large and flexible repertoire of vocal, facial, and other outward expressions that demonstrate an awareness of verbal and nonverbal behavioral responses in other cultures.

Effective teachers of Black children have to (1) be aware of cultural influences in cross-cultural interactions and reflect on their assumptions about Black children's culture—especially assumptions regarding cultural deficits; (2) acquire knowledge about their own cultural preferences, practices, norms, and conventions and those of Black children; (3) direct energy and attention toward learning about the strengths and preferences of other cultures, while expecting that they will function well in those cultures; and (4) employ actions (vocal, facial, and other expressions) that demonstrate an awareness of verbal and nonverbal behavioral responses in Black culture. In a classroom setting it is the grown-up who should have the higher level of cultural intelligence, not the child. It is the teacher's responsibility to adjust to and understand the child's cultural expectations and preferences. No child should keep getting into trouble until she figures out the teacher's cultural expectations and preferences.

It goes without saying that some people have a higher level of cultural intelligence than others and are more adept at navigating cross-cultural interactions. This would be the case with any form of intelligence. However, it also goes without saying that anyone can increase his level of cultural intelligence through awareness, knowledge, energy, and action. The first step is simply to respect differences between cultures by suspending judgment and by questioning your assumptions about Black culture. The second step is to be confident in your ability to learn more about Black culture and use what you learn to increase your ability to educate Black children.

▎ THE RELATIONSHIP BETWEEN TEACHER EFFICACY AND ACHIEVEMENT

Efficacy is the capacity for producing a desired result or effect even when faced with challenges. Self-efficacy is your belief in your own ability and capacity to produce a desired result or to deal with any challenges you may face. Therefore, *teacher efficacy* can be defined as a teacher's belief in her ability to successfully affect children's academic performance in spite of any challenges that may arise. Teacher efficacy is related to cultural intelligence in that teachers must feel confident that they can be effective in culturally diverse situations, and as every teacher knows, the way to increase confidence in the ability to understand, integrate, and apply new knowledge successfully is through continued education and practice.

As the dean of Pacific Oaks College Northwest (PONW), I was regularly amazed at the number of pre-service teachers (early childhood and K–8) who were thoroughly convinced that (1) they could not be successful teaching Black children or that (2) Black children had so many barriers and obstacles to overcome that learning would always be a struggle for them. As is true with any self-fulfilling prophecy, if teachers believe they cannot teach Black children, then they will not be able to do so, and if teachers believe Black children struggle as learners, then Black children will continue to do so. The research is clear that teacher efficacy is directly related to student achievement and that highly efficacious teachers produce high academic achievement with Black children (Ferguson 2003; Goddard, Hoy, and Hoy 2000; Goodwin 2010/2011; Haberman 1995; Muijs and Reynolds 2002).

When my daughter was in the fourth grade, her class was preparing to take the Washington Assessment of Student Learning (WASL), which is a test administered statewide to all students. The school spent months preparing the fourth graders for the test. When she came home on testing day, she asked, "Why was my teacher so afraid of the WASL? It wasn't that hard." Interestingly, this happened in a K–8 Catholic school, and some research indicates that Catholic schools have been found to be more effective in teaching Black children than public schools (Bryk, Lee, and Holland 1993; Shields 1989; York 1996). We all must be very intentional in using strategies to resist unconscious or subconscious beliefs about our ability to effectively educate every child because even teachers who are otherwise highly qualified may lack confidence in their ability to be successful with Black children (Pang and Sablan, 1998). Fortunately, there are ways to reflect on your own level of confidence and to increase that confidence by increasing cultural intelligence.

▶ INCORPORATING CULTURAL INFLUENCES INTO TEACHING AND LEARNING

When I think about cultural competency, cultural relevancy, and teachers in a classroom filled with diversity, I think of cooking in my kitchen. Those who know me know I have a love affair with food and I love to cook. I probably have 150 cookbooks representing just about every aspect of cooking possible: from Ethiopia to Thailand, from the vegetarian's delight to the carnivore's heaven, from cooking with children to cooking with Julia Child, from soups to sambals, from brunch to bean banquets, from slow roasting to flash frying, from . . . well, you get the point. When I come home from work, I like nothing better than to survey the fridge, the pantry, the cabinets, and the herb garden to see what I can concoct with what is on hand. If you come for dinner, you might have chicken marinated in leftover pickle juice—or it could be potatoes tossed with Habesha berbere—or maybe French-baked cucumbers with Indian masoor dal—or perhaps shrimp and corn sautéed with herbs from my backyard.

Teaching in a classroom with a broad diversity of children can be a very similar experience. Having knowledge of more learning styles, multiple intelligences, and personality types/traits is like having the knowledge of 150 cookbooks at your disposal. No matter how many different cultures are in your classroom any given year, if you are deeply familiar with your own culture and the cultures of your children, you can produce a curriculum that draws on many different sources and is relevant to many of the children you have the honor of teaching. Knowing more about Black culture will add valuable elements to your "pantry"!

▶ AFRICENTRIC CURRICULUM AND TEACHER EFFICACY

Both children and grown-ups are more engaged when content is relevant to their lives and their cultures. Teachers will have children representing numerous cultures in their classrooms, and their effectiveness with all of them increases when those cultures are woven into the teaching and learning experience—when those cultures are used to scaffold learning (Vygotsky 1978). You increase your cultural intelligence by becoming more familiar with students from different backgrounds and understanding the perspectives of each child. An African- or African American–centered curriculum will increase Black children's engagement with the content and the learning process.

The goal when teaching Black children is to understand and work within the norms of the Black social, cultural, historical, and current reality. When teaching African American children, this also means giving deep and reflective thought to how you approach topics such as enslavement, discrimination, and prejudice. It is important to acknowledge and address the inequities and challenges Black children may face. Giving children the message that they are too young to explore these issues tells them you either don't know or don't care about their experiences and the experiences of the people in their families and communities.

Of course the challenge for many teachers is that most teacher preparation programs do not adequately provide future teachers with the expertise or knowledge to effectively incorporate diverse cultural influences into the learning process. Asa Hilliard (1995b) described some of our teacher training approaches as bordering on professional malpractice because they fail to provide information about the real children future teachers would actually have in their classrooms. Very few teachers will be in classrooms with textbook children. For many of the pre-service teachers I worked with at PONW, their first contact with Black culture was with the Black children in their classrooms. Many of them had not grown up around people of African descent and knew very little about them except what they heard from the media or from others. Having a deeper understanding of Black culture will increase teacher efficacy because, for most of us, the more we know about something, the more confident we feel about engaging with it.

The Iceberg Model of Culture can help you begin to gain that understanding and increase your confidence. Introduced by Edward T. Hall in 1976, the Iceberg Model of Culture says that what you see at the surface level tells you very little about a culture. According to the model, every culture has three levels—surface culture, deep culture, and unconscious culture—but the one that shows up most often in a culture-centric curriculum is surface culture. This means the focus is on cultural elements that are easily seen, identified, and accessed (food, dress, music, art, crafts, dance, literature, language, celebrations, games). In an Africentric preschool curriculum operating at the surface level you will find pictures of Africans and African Americans, African or African American music, traditional foods, a map of the continent, games like mancala, celebrations of important events such as Kwanzaa and Juneteenth, and images of people such as Martin Luther King Jr. While it is important to incorporate these elements into Black children's learning environments, to make learning more meaningful and relevant, and to increase active engagement, you must go beneath the surface. The surface culture is a good place to start in changing *curriculum* in visual ways. To change *pedagogy*, however, requires an increased knowledge of the other two levels of culture:

Deep Culture is behavior-based (courtesy, conduct, concepts of time, personal space, facial expressions, body language, eye contact, touching).

Unconscious Culture is values-based (notions and concepts of leadership, modesty, marriage, family, child rearing, elders, kinship, gender, class, decision making, problem solving).

Strategies and methods for changing both curriculum and pedagogy will be covered more fully in chapters 5 through 7. What you need to do at this stage is increase your ability to recognize the elements of each level within your own culture and the impact they have on *your* teaching and learning preferences. This will make it easier for you to understand the role and importance of cultural elements in other cultures and the ways in which children's cultures impact their learning preferences. Sooner than you might think, you will have increased your ability to create a learning environment that incorporates the cultural experiences of Black children, increased their active engagement with learning tasks at hand, increased their task performance, and *decreased* the academic achievement gap. Now it's time for part 2 and putting all of this into practice.

PART 2

PUTTING IT INTO PRACTICE

When I ask grown-ups about their vision for the children who will be leaders in 2030, I get a list of characteristics, skills, abilities, and approaches that are considered vital for leadership. My follow-up question is, "At what age do we expect children to learn and apply these leadership traits?" Often we appear to be describing future leaders who do all the things we don't allow in many of our early learning environments. I think part of the challenge is remembering that education is not just about passing a test. It's about growing as a person. I liken it to the fact that many of us may have learned enough French to pass our French tests all those years ago, but few of us actually speak French today.[1] If Black children are to become the leaders we want them to be, we must let them do those things that nurture leadership skills and abilities. We must cultivate their genius. In part 2, we will look at how we make that happen—how we put into place practices to create learning environments that help us accomplish the growth and development Black children need to be successful academically, personally, and professionally.

● ● ●

---

[1] Yes, I *did* keep studying and using French, most recently in Paris in summer of 2013.

CHAPTER 4

Key Elements of Appropriate Learning Environments for Children of African Descent

Now that we've reviewed the learning styles, intelligences, and personality types/traits that are found in many Black children and looked at the cultural contexts of learning, it's time to consider some of the elements of a learning environment that would best support their academic achievement and expand their opportunities to reach their full potential. This list is not exhaustive, but it can serve as a good place to start. Of course, incorporating these elements into the learning environment will benefit all students who share similar learning preferences. It's important to clarify again that identifying the learning preferences of any group of children should not be used to stereotype that group. The goal here is to gradually increase elements that will lead to a classroom where all children's learning needs can be addressed.

Based on my consideration of the research previously presented, I would say that many Black children learn best in an environment with the following elements:

- active, engaged, synergetic learning
- interactive discourse, discussion, and analysis with an emphasis on verbal "play"
- opportunities for creativity, individualism, and embellishment
- collective/collaborative activity and problem solving
- competitive mental and physical challenges
- meaningful, mutually respectful teacher-child relationship

- meaningful, mutually respectful connection to family and community
- educational empowerment/personal responsibility
- opportunities for self-reflection
- opportunities for connecting with nature and each other for a higher purpose or a good cause
- an integrated, connected curriculum
- a sense of community and belonging

For each of these twelve elements, I will provide a strategy for implementation and examples for different ages. You'll be impressed by what happens when Black children get to do the things noted here. The tables below categorize the age groups as follows:

EC: early childhood (ages 2–3)
PS: preschool (ages 3–4)
K1: kindergarten/first grade (ages 5–6)
G23: second/third grades (ages 6–8)

Active, Engaged Learning

STRATEGY	EXAMPLE
Ensure ample time to "work" (play).	**EC:** Allow an amount of unstructured time for young children to engage in pretend play, alone and with each other. This can be a good 15–20 minutes for this age. **PS:** The time can be more structured in the sense that children may be selecting specific areas of the classroom in which to work. For this group, 30–45 minutes should be provided. **K1:** At this age, children's work may be more task oriented, but there still needs to be ample time for them to really engage with the learning. One example is 30 minutes offered three times per week. **G23:** For older children, this element can be group projects on which they have an hour each week to work.
Provide time for children to follow their own interests and tailor your activities and centers to their interests and abilities.	**EC:** Many young children really like to explore "packaging," so have a space for boxes, bags (not plastic!), and containers. **PS:** Many children like "junk," so provide an area where they can take apart and explore safe items. **K1:** Monthly themes work well here. Just let the children choose the themes that interest them. **G23:** Let children pick longer projects to work on throughout the year.

Active, Engaged Learning
continued

STRATEGY	EXAMPLE
Incorporate ample opportunities to move around the learning environment.	**EC:** Provide learning activities that require standing up, marching, dancing. **PS:** If your classroom has centers, move the group from center to center for some learning activities. **K1:** Every 20 minutes or so, incorporate a "station break" when the children go to stations or centers to complete tasks. **G23:** Have tables and theme areas that students can use during the day (such as a "math concepts" table).
Incorporate more "self-talk" and peer tutoring into learning activities.	**EC:** Just let them talk and see what they say. **PS:** Ask children to say what they are doing as they do it. **K1:** Have different children be the "teacher" for small groups. **G23:** Create "learning buddies" by pairing a child who knows a bit more about the task with one who's not quite there yet.
Create an actively engaging learning environment with mentally stimulating visuals and materials.	**EC:** Have culturally relevant patterns, fabrics, toys, and games in the learning environment. **PS:** Have pictures of the children's families in the classroom. **K1:** Have "puzzle time" with both board puzzles and manipulative puzzles. **G23:** Put optical illusions on the walls and change them monthly.
Let children touch stuff and have plenty of things for them to touch.	**EC/PS:** Provide *tons* of items and materials for experiential, hands-on opportunities. Change textures, sizes, colors regularly. **K1/G23:** Severely limit the amount of items in the room that are "for teacher only." Every classroom should have more for the children than it does for the teacher.
Provide opportunities for a synergetic learning environment where more than one thing may be happening at the same time.	**EC:** This will happen regularly during free time for pretend play. **PS:** Have low-volume music playing at various times during the day. **K1/G23:** Put children in groups of three to complete some learning tasks simultaneously.

Interactive Discourse, Discussion, and Analysis with an Emphasis on Verbal "Play"

STRATEGY	EXAMPLE
Create many opportunities for children to discuss what they're learning with each other.	**EC:** Look for parallel play and serve as the "conversation bridge" between the students. **PS:** Have children pair up during "work" time. **K1/G23:** Have numerous paired or small-group discussions during the day.
Respond to children's statements and questions with increasingly complex conversations.	**EC:** I go outside./Do you want to go outside now? **PS:** Is it my turn?/I think you could be next. **K1:** What is this called?/I believe that is called a mandolin. **G23:** Yesterday I went to the zoo./That sounds like an incredibly exciting venture.
Connect children's reading to their interests, not just their reading level.	**EC:** Provide lots of nonfiction picture books that cover lots of different topics. **PS:** Change the books in the classroom regularly and vary the topics. **K1:** Ask them what they are interested in and provide books about those topics. **G23:** Let them read comic books if they want. It's reading!
Incorporate verbal activities such as debate, speech, imagery, and creative storytelling.	**EC:** Tell stories without using a book. **PS:** Throughout the week, let each child tell a story. **K1:** Have weekly debates. **G23:** Listen to how children use language in their conversations with each other and point out their usage of metaphor, hyperbole, or wordplay.
Provide opportunities for wordplay through riddles, paradoxes, jokes, proverbs, and limericks.	**EC:** Have "rhyme" day where you ask children to say a word and then you say, "that rhymes with . . ." **PS:** Read books by authors such as Dr. Seuss to the class. **K1:** Have children create their own riddles. **G23:** Give children a paradox on Monday to think about and then discuss it on Friday.
Encourage colorful, playful, inventive language.	**EC:** Have children engage in pretend play. Listen to what they say and build on that language. **PS:** Have children make up silly stories. **K1:** Create a "class language." **G23:** Give children a sentence and have them add more and more adjectives.
Provide opportunities for children to learn a second language, perhaps even an African language.	**EC:** Teach them how to count to 10 in an African language. **PS:** Label some classroom items in an African language. **K1:** Teach them "Nkosi sikelel' iAfrika," the South African national anthem. **G23:** Ask them for a list of words they would like to learn in an African language.
Support respect for home language/dialect while providing lots of opportunities for children to increase their use of standard, academic English.	For all ages, use what I call the "affirming restating" approach without telling children they are saying it wrong. For example, if a child says, "She be hungry all the time," you can affirm and restate by saying, "Yes, she is often hungry."

Interactive Discourse, Discussion, and Analysis with an Emphasis on Verbal "Play"

continued

STRATEGY	EXAMPLE
Provide opportunities for generating ideas orally and visually in addition to writing them down.	**EC:** Tell me what you did today. **PS:** Draw a picture of what you did. **K1:** Describe how you got that answer. **G23:** Tell me what you think this science project is about.
Ask open-ended questions that require more than a yes/no, one-word answer.	**EC:** Why is this your favorite toy? **PS:** How do you think milk gets into our milk cartons? **K1:** What do you think will happen if we mix these two things together? **G23:** Why is it important for us to respect each other?

Opportunities for Creativity, Individualism, and Embellishment

STRATEGY	EXAMPLE
Let each child grow in her strength areas.	For younger children, discover what each one is really good at and let her do that often. For older children, ask them what they are good at and how you can help them be even better.
Provide opportunities for children to express themselves in creative, unstructured, self-defined ways through language, emotions, and gestures.	**EC:** Take pictures of the students expressing different emotions for a discussion about feelings. **PS:** Have them draw pictures that describe what they are feeling or thinking. **K1:** Have them create songs that describe exciting events. **G23:** Have them create a play that describes their class.
Let children embellish a predetermined task.	**EC:** Let them color their pictures with whatever colors they wish. Who says you can't have a purple banana? **PS:** Give them the first part of a sentence and let them finish it however they choose. **K1:** Start a story and let each child finish it his own way. **G23:** Start a song and let each child create the rest of the verses.
Let each child be an individual.	**EC:** Ask children to name one yummy thing and one yucky thing. **PS:** Ask them to name something unique about themselves. **K1:** Ask them to name something unique about each other. **G23:** Have them talk about their favorite hobby.
"Destructure" the arts. All of them have become increasingly restrictive.	**EC/PS:** Put out age-appropriate multimedia materials at the same time (paints, pipe cleaners, geometric shapes, glue, tape, scissors, recyclables). **K1/G23:** Have each child choose a favorite song and come up with all new verses or reword the current ones.

Collective/Collaborative Activity and Problem Solving

STRATEGY	EXAMPLE
Provide activities that incorporate creative problem solving.	**EC:** Have a "What is it?" day when you bring something intriguing (a large binder clip or a baby bottle scrubber) and ask children what it's used for. **PS:** Ask children what it would take to have a pet giraffe. **K1:** Have children build their own Lego animals. **G23:** Have children present problems they would like to solve and then come up with their own solutions.
Allow plenty of opportunities for critical analysis.	For many age groups, simply incorporating "why" throughout the day is a good beginning. For example, why is it important to clean up? Why do you think we have class rules? Why did all the dinosaurs die? Why do plants need sunshine? Don't look for "right" and "wrong" answers. The goal is to have children think, debate, ponder, and question.
Use students' misconceptions/ mistakes as opportunities for deeper learning.	**EC:** It didn't work that time, so let's try again. **PS:** What can you do differently this time? **K1:** Pour the water into the other container and see if the two are the same size. **G23:** What other letters might make the sounds in that word?
Incorporate the scientific method by using studies and projects.	**EC/PS:** Select a geometric shape and spend a month finding it inside and outside the classroom, drawing it, making things with it, and playing with it. **K1:** Use the task of "using the alphabet to read and write" as a way to study global writing systems. **G23:** Select a yearlong theme (like aviation or homes) and tie all curriculum (math, reading, art, language) to that theme.
Let children take responsibility for their own conflict resolution and provide examples of peaceful resolutions.	**EC:** What will make you feel better? **PS:** What will make you both feel better? **K1:** What can you do to make sure everyone feels good? **G23:** Let me know how the two of you would like to resolve this.
Let children learn from each other.	**EC:** Observe how kids "copy" each other (using a pencil or learning a new word) and create opportunities for them to do it more. **PS/K1:** Have two children complete a task together. **G23:** Try a "teach-discuss-task" approach that has children talk about content in large and small groups on a regular basis.

Competitive Mental and Physical Challenges

STRATEGY	EXAMPLE
Create opportunities for critical reasoning and critical thinking.	**EC:** Have "Which ones go together?" days and incorporate a variety of items and materials. **PS:** Give children a large group of items and materials and have them make "sets." **K1:** After reading a story, ask children why they think different characters did what they did. **G23:** Have weekly "Figure it out" days. Give children a tough problem to solve and have them spend an hour engaging with it in small groups of two or three.
Make sure learning activities let children progress from remembering to understanding to applying to analyzing to evaluating to creating.	**EC:** Where do the blocks belong? **PS:** Why do we put the blocks away? **K1:** What is the best way to put away our materials? **G23:** How should our classroom be organized so that we use it the best way?
Incorporate mentally challenging activities.	**EC:** picture puzzles **PS:** tangram puzzles **K1:** checkers **G23:** chess
Let children be little scientists, explorers, inventors, and creators.	**EC:** Have lots of conversations about the weather throughout the day and the week. **PS:** Have a variety of materials for them to construct and "destruct." **K1:** Grow different plants from seeds. **G23:** Take a marine biology field trip to a site with hands-on activities.
Provide ample opportunities for physical activity, dance, and other forms of movement.	**EC:** Teach simple sign language (signs for more, girl, boy, food). **PS:** Teach finger spelling while teaching the alphabet. **K1:** Teach children songs in sign language. **G23:** Have children create their own sign language for classroom use—a "secret" language.
Provide critiques (not criticisms) of mental and physical performance that include useful strategies for improvement.	**EC:** I see you're trying to put in the last puzzle piece. What if you turn it another way? **PS:** I see you are using a lot of blocks to build that bridge. What if you put the bigger ones on the bottom? **K1:** I see you are trying to add all the numbers in your head. What if you use your fingers to add them up? **G23:** I see you are trying to run faster. What if you try holding your head straight up?
Build on students' pride in overcoming obstacles and barriers to success in mental and physical challenges.	**EC:** I think you should try again. **PS:** What else can you try? **K1:** I see that you know more about this today than you did yesterday. **G23:** I think you will know more about this tomorrow than you do today.
Let children create their own tests of their learning and physical challenges/competitions.	**EC:** Ask how they know who runs faster. **PS:** Let them create their own athletic events. **K1:** Have them show you how they know they've learned something. **G23:** Let them create the test that the class will take (how many different ways can our group represent 256?).

Meaningful, Mutually Respectful Teacher-Child Relationship

STRATEGY	EXAMPLE
Build on children's interpersonal, relationship-based preferences by ensuring that you, the teacher, are part of the "team" and not a nonparticipant in the learning experience.	**EC:** Use "we" and "our" in your conversations. **PS:** Share stories about yourself as a child. **K1:** Create occasions for you to put your desk in the center of a student semicircle. **G23:** Incorporate what children already know into the learning activity. Spend time asking each child.
Get to know children and let them get to know you.	**EC:** Share day-to-day practices such as what you like to eat and your favorite games. **PS:** Share stories about special occasions and holi-/holy days. **K1/G23:** You should know at least one wonderfully unique thing about every child, something you wouldn't know from looking at a file.
Let children talk, and listen to what they have to say.	Teachers spend too much time talking. In almost any learning activity at almost any age, let children talk by asking questions or letting them describe something. Then, write down what they say and find ways to incorporate that information into the activity so they know you were listening to them.
See every child in a nonschool context.	**EC:** Frequent the park where they play or the grocery store where they shop so they see you outside of the classroom. **PS:** Accept invitations to their nonschool birthday parties. **K1/G23:** Attend their weekend dance recitals, sports events, martial arts competitions, community events.

Meaningful, Mutually Respectful Connection to Family and Community

STRATEGY	EXAMPLE
Build on African Americans' strong sense of connection between heritage and history.	**EC:** Have pictures of children's families, friends, and community members in the classroom. **PS:** Ask children what's special about their various family members. **K1:** Talk about your own culture and ask them about theirs. **G23:** Talk about Black people outside of enslavement by incorporating the history of ancient African empires and the strengths and achievements of their current community and the nation.
Connect new learning to what children already know as individuals, within their families, in their community, and in their history.	With young children, let families know what you are teaching and ask them what their children already know about the topics. With older children, just ask them what they already know about the topic and how that does or does not connect with their own experiences and the experiences of people they know.
Get to know each family's expectations for their children.	**EC:** Ask families what excites, motivates, comforts, and frustrates each child. **PS:** Ask families about the learning strengths of their children. **K1:** Develop an annual learning plan with families—discuss what they want their children to learn and what you want their children to learn. **G23:** Work with children and families to determine each child's learning style, multiple intelligences, and personality type and see if these are being addressed in the learning environment.
Get to know each child's community.	**EC:** Schedule home visits early in the school year. **PS:** Familiarize yourself with the stores, libraries, places of worship, and community centers where your young students might be when school is out. **K1:** Learn more about the special events and occasions that are important in the Black community so you can talk about them in the classroom. **G23:** Attend special events and occasions that are important in the Black community.

Educational Empowerment/Personal Responsibility

STRATEGY	EXAMPLE
Provide opportunities for children to make many choices.	**EC:** Have a variety of nutritious foods available for snack and let children select what they want to eat. **PS:** Put out a broad variety of science materials and let children engage with them as they choose. **K1:** Have more than one way to approach a learning activity and let each child choose. For example, a math activity might be numbers on paper, beads in cups, a made-up song, or a story. **G23:** Let children rotate between different, but conflicting, values (one winner or many winners, having the most or sharing the most, and so on).
Allow time for children to plan their own learning.	**EC:** Ask them what they want to do. **PS:** Ask them what they want to learn. **K1:** Ask them how they want to learn a new topic. **G23:** Ask them to outline the steps they will use to approach a reading project.
Provide opportunities for children to choose what to learn.	**EC:** Interest areas should have a broad variety of items and materials that contribute to the learning goal so that any choice will be effective. **PS:** Provide a choice of three different learning activities and let children engage with them in the order they prefer. **K1:** For free time, have fun and exciting games that meet learning objectives. **G23:** If children are learning another language, let them provide the vocabulary list of the words they want to learn first.
Encourage and incorporate opportunities for independent action and self-sufficiency.	**EC:** Do not rush in to help when a child is not accomplishing something right away. **PS:** When you do step in to help, ask the child what he has already done and encourage more attempts if there has only been one. **K1:** Have a class rule that children must attempt something three times before seeking help from the teacher. **G23:** Have children track, monitor, and analyze their own points and progress throughout the week and let them earn extra points if they need them.

Opportunities for Self-Reflection

STRATEGY	EXAMPLE
Let children think about their strengths.	**EC:** What do you like to do most? **PS:** What are you really good at? **K1:** What's your favorite subject in school and why? **G23:** What strength do you bring to our learning community?
Allow ample time for thinking, just thinking.	**EC:** Provide "thinking breaks" of 10–15 seconds. Then, ask each child what he or she thought about. **PS:** Increase the time to a minute. **K1:** Have children say what they want to think about and provide 2–3 minutes to do so. **G23:** Give a topic to think about and provide 3–5 minutes to do so.
Create opportunities for *productive* self-reflection in a conflict. No "time out"!	**EC:** How are you feeling right now? **PS:** What could you do to make this better? **K1:** How can we use our class rules here? **G23:** What could you have done to prevent this from happening?
Use every opportunity possible for incorporating decision-making skills.	**EC:** Every day have a different child pick the song to be sung. **PS:** Every day have a different child describe what the weather is like. **K1:** Every child contributes in deciding class rules. **G23:** When things don't go as planned, let the children decide the next step.
Use inquiry-based, discovery learning to integrate core content with children's pursuits of their own questions.	**EC:** Discuss trees and leaves and then go on an "ask a question" nature walk. **PS/K1:** Pick a topic, such as fabric, and have children ask their own questions about it. Spend time uncovering the answers. **G23:** Ask children for questions they have and spend the year letting them find the answer.
Discuss the role of the wise elders in traditional African society, who are often described as very reflective thinkers.	**EC:** Ask children who is the smartest grown-up they know and why. **PS:** Ask the same question and have them say what that person has said that they like. **K1:** Read stories about African and African American proverbs. **G23:** Ask children about the wise grown-ups they know and teach them about the role of the African griots.

Opportunities for Connecting with Nature and Each Other for a Higher Purpose or a Good Cause

STRATEGY	EXAMPLE
Provide opportunities for children to connect with the plant world.	**EC:** Grow a plant from seed and talk about it weekly. **PS:** Have children choose a plant that interests them and create monthly activities that include it. **K1:** Grow edible plants in small containers outside. **G23:** Spend a year learning about how food gets from the farm to their tables.
Provide opportunities for children to connect with the animal world.	**EC/PS:** Read stories about a wide variety of animals (extinct, living, and pretend). **K1:** Visit a local zoo and discuss what it takes to care for animals, including pets. **G23:** Have each child select an animal or species to study in-depth.
Provide opportunities for children to connect with the local human world.	**EC:** Learn five phrases in the languages of the African children in your class (hello, good-bye, thank you, you're welcome). **PS:** Let children who speak the same language work together. **K1:** Have children select home language words to teach their classmates. **G23:** Have students learn songs sung by the African children in your class.
Provide opportunities for children to connect with the global human world.	**EC:** Have pictures of *current* Black leaders, scientists, and authors from around the world. **PS:** Have a map that shows all the places on the planet (not just the U.S. and Africa) where people of African descent live. **K1:** Teach children about *current* Black leaders, scientists, and authors from around the world. **G23:** Teach children about Black people around the world who have won Nobel prizes.
Provide opportunities for children to participate in service activities.	**EC:** Each week have them do something helpful for a classmate. **PS:** Have them create a group service project for their classroom. **K1:** Have them create a service project for their school. **G23:** Have them create or participate in a service project for the community.
Incorporate more opportunities around gardening, recycling, community development, and sustainability.	**EC:** Go on a nature walk around your area and have children talk about what they see. **PS:** Have children bring in recyclables for an art project. **K1:** Have children develop recycling activities for their classroom. **G23:** Have children develop activities that increase recycling in their community.
Provide more activities that include meteorology, geography, botany, marine science, ecology, and other sciences.	**EC:** Have children discuss the weather they like most and why. **PS:** Have children make maps of their classroom or school. **K1:** Have children learn and identify different trees in their community. **G23:** Have children create a garden out of plastic bottles of all sizes.

An Integrated, Connected Curriculum

STRATEGY	EXAMPLE
Ensure that learning activities are interconnected and presented in a holistic way.	**EC:** Decide on a single focus (like the color red) and incorporate it throughout the day and week. **PS:** With any activity, ask children how it connects to their lives. **K1:** Use themes to weave in all learning and activities. **G23:** Use mind maps to link a variety of content and activities.
Employ the "big picture" method of a subject to show where the learning task or activity is headed.	**EC:** Sing the ABC song while pointing to the letters. **PS:** We're going to learn the 26 letters of the alphabet. "A" is the first one. **K1:** We're going to use this map of our school building to learn about north, south, east, and west. **G23:** A "habitat" is where someone lives. Some people live indoors and some live outdoors. We're going to look at different animal habitats.
Weave annual academic content into a single theme, study, or project.	**EC:** Use emotions to discuss math (graphs of daily feelings), literacy (expressions with words attached), and language (learning to name various feelings in the languages of other children in the classroom). **PS/K1:** Use picture-based mind maps of what will be covered and find out what questions children have. **G23:** Create word-based mind maps and let children add what related items interest them.

A Sense of Community and Belonging

STRATEGY	EXAMPLE
Make sure every child is included. Watch for the overlooked and the "hiders."	**EC:** Arrange tables in a semicircle with you at the center. **PS:** Seat children in groups of 3 or 4 and give each one a task or responsibility. **K1:** Have children create character cards for each other. **G23:** Create a schedule to ensure you have positive interactions with each child equally during the week.
Let children do things together.	**EC:** Create ways for children to play or work together, and keep an eye out for anyone who is left out. **PS/K1:** "Mix and match" children regularly so they get to know everyone in the class. **G23:** Create "family groups" or "prides" within the classroom, maybe even mixed-age groups within the school, to replicate having siblings.
Create a caring community where children are expected to care for each other even when they aren't getting along.	**EC:** Have a "share" day when children have to share classroom items. **PS:** Let children create their own rules for how to share. **K1:** Have children create rules for resolving conflicts. **G23:** Create communal discernment groups for resolving conflict.

As I thought of these examples, I drew on my own experiences as a child and what I would have liked to see; the experiences of my three children when they were young; and my observations of and interactions with my grandson who was two to three years old as I was writing this book. Each of us did better in school when the learning environments resembled what I've described here. When these elements were not in place, we tended to be bored, antsy, detached, resigned, in trouble, or frustrated—or as my grandson said when he was two and a half, "I'm so fruterated!" Often the children presenting these behaviors in classrooms are the ones most in need of more cognitive challenge. Nothing suggested here is undoable. Sure, it may take time to learn to count to ten in Tigrinya, but my grandson could count to ten in Portuguese (the latest language I'm learning) and to twelve or thirteen in Spanish before he was three years old. We just have to be strategic and intentional about changing how we teach Black children, changing the learning environment we create for Black children, and changing our relationships with Black children, their families, and their communities.

CHAPTER 5

Changing the Teaching and Learning Environment

W HAT DOES IT MEAN TO CHANGE the teaching and learning environment? For starters, it does not mean throwing everything you learned in your teacher preparation program out the window. Changing the teaching and learning environment is actually about bringing in more of what you learned. It's about being able to understand and articulate how Black children are learning, knowing that how they are learning may look different from what you are used to seeing or what you are expecting to see. When teachers are deeply familiar with their learning goals and outcomes, they know there are a lot of ways for children to demonstrate success. By incorporating more of the learning styles, multiple intelligences, and personality types/traits into teaching and learning, teachers will have many ways to demonstrate that Black children are meeting those learning goals and outcomes. If "all roads lead to Rome," there should be more than one way to get there. It's about sharing—sharing goals and expectations, sharing power and control, sharing discourse and ideas, sharing the room, sharing the daily routine, and sharing classroom management.

▶ SHARING GOALS AND EXPECTATIONS

I hear it time and again: parents are children's first teachers. Teachers usually consult with each other regarding student expectations and challenging students to achieve more; however, effective teaching requires teachers to have these conversations with parents when it comes to social-emotional and academic goals for Black children. Consulting with the first teacher means sharing goals around high expectations, academic challenge, and learning outcomes. Black parents, like all parents, want their children to do well in school, and they have high expectations for their children's academic success. They may not always know how to make that happen themselves, but I have not met one Black parent who has "academic failure" as a goal for their child. Effective teachers of Black children consult with parents and incorporate parental expectations into their teaching at the beginning of each school year.

When the teacher's goals and expectations don't match those of the parent, children are bound to be stuck in the middle. My father had very high expectations of his children when it came to school. His motto was, "Don't give me 95 percent when I ask for 100 percent." That meant that he expected me to do schoolwork over if I didn't achieve 100 percent. Every Friday night was "School Night," and my father would create schoolwork for me and my siblings that we would have to work on and study for two hours. As we got older, School Night got harder. In *school*, however, it was a very different story, and it became obvious my teachers had lower expectations. In kindergarten, I actually got into trouble for bringing a book for show-and-tell that was at a reading level higher than the *Dick and Jane* books my classmates were reading. My teacher told me that reading such books in front of the other children made them feel bad about themselves and that I could read *Dick and Jane* like everyone else or nothing at all (yes, a true story). In fourth grade, in a different school with a different teacher, I was asked to stay away from the color-coded, go-at-your-own-pace reading boxes (SRA Reading Laboratory for those who remember) for two weeks because I was getting too far ahead of the rest of the class. There were so many other instances with different teachers, in different schools, even in different cities! My father challenged me to make "A" grades in every subject, every time. Yet I don't recall that any of my teachers ever consulted with him or my mother about their goals and expectations for me.

Of course, I too wanted to challenge myself. And that's what complicates matters further: children also have learning goals. Many Black children entering preschool or kindergarten have goals and expectations of their own. When my daughter started kindergarten, she already had in her head what she expected to learn. After two weeks of school, she came home annoyed. When I asked what was wrong, she said there were kids in her class who knew their "teens," and she couldn't understand why her preschool teacher hadn't taught her the "teens"—the teacher must have known my daughter would need to know the "teens" in kindergarten. The majority of children are smarter and more aware of what grown-ups are thinking than we give them credit for. Children know what we expect (or don't expect) of them. For whatever reason, most of my teachers were reluctant to challenge me and hold me to high expectations, and they did not want me to challenge myself or have high expectations for myself. They did not know how to share academic learning goals and expectations.

What you do:

- Ask parents about their academic expectations for their children.
- Ask parents how best to challenge their children to increase academic performance.
- Ask children about their academic expectations and goals for themselves.
- Assume that the Black children in your classroom are geniuses.

What children do:

- They tell you what they want to learn.
- They review their learning progress on a regular basis.
- They provide suggestions as to what might help them learn better.
- They tell you how they would like to be challenged, and how they would like to learn more.

How it looks:

- It's obvious to all that you, the parents, and the children are working toward the same goals.
- You document collaborative learning goals in ways that are easily understood by all parties involved.
- You, the children, and the parents have daily casual conversations, outside of parent-teacher conferences, about each child's learning and progress.
- You have an active and engaged positive daily interaction with each Black child.

How it sounds:

- It's noisy at times because you and the children are energetically pursuing shared learning goals and expectations.
- Children are actively pursuing their passionate interests to meet their learning expectations.
- Children are talking with each other about what they are learning.
- You are asking children what they are learning and how well they think they are learning it.

How it feels:

- You may feel a little preliminary awkwardness about asking children what they expect to learn and how.
- Children feel excited about getting down to the business of learning what they expect to learn.
- You feel excited and motivated by your initial conversations with parents.
- You, the parents, and the children feel you are all on the same team pursuing shared goals.

How it's structured:

- You consult with parents at the beginning of the school year.
- You consult with children at the beginning of the school year.
- You build in ways to challenge children to higher levels of learning by looking for opportunities to build on current levels.
- You have biweekly, more formal consultations (not "conferences") with parents and children to track academic progress. No one wants to hear at the end of the term that academic progress is not being made.

◗ SHARING POWER AND CONTROL

For many teachers, the notion of sharing power and control with children in the classroom is either foreign or frightening. It's not that all teachers are power hungry (although some really are). It's just that our stereotypical idea of teaching does not usually include children having control. Sharing power and control with children does not mean creating a totally chaotic learning environment. That would be a pendulum swing to the other extreme—which is not sharing. But teachers have power and control over too many things, too much of the time. Teachers decide:

- who speaks, how long, and how often
- the pace of the day, what will be covered, and what will be cut
- what children can touch and use and how they are to touch and use it
- who they expect will perform well and who will not
- to whom children can talk and for how long
- what children should look at ("See the bird?") rather than asking them what they see
- when children can sharpen a pencil or get a tissue
- how children should resolve their disagreements
- when children *should* be ready for the next step instead of asking if they *are* ready

The list goes on. Now, this doesn't mean that teachers should never decide these things. It just means that teachers don't have to *always* decide these things. Teachers have daily opportunities to share power and control in small, yet extremely meaningful ways with children. The question you may be asking right now is, "Why?" Why should children have some power and control? To me, the answer is simple: because it's *their* education and they should have opportunities to take some responsibility for it. Black children *want* some ownership over their education; they *want* to participate. Teachers want students to have ownership, responsibility, and participation when it comes to learning. Yet we often want children to develop skills and abilities without our being intentional about how and when we give them the opportunities to do so.

Sharing power with children means stepping back and giving them the time and the space to do the things we want them to do, to not be afraid of just observing or listening. Once I was coaching a new teacher, and she put a sentence on the board for her class of four-year-olds to copy. While they were doing this, she and I were standing to the side having a quiet conversation. After about five minutes, the children slowly began talking, not loudly, but definitely talking.

> TEACHER: Room D, I need you to quiet down and get back to work.
> ME: I'm curious why you told them to stop talking.
> TEACHER: I wanted them to focus on writing.
> ME: How do you know they weren't focused on writing?
> TEACHER: I have no idea! I don't even know what they were saying!

I pointed out to her that some of the children could have been engaging in self-talk, coaching themselves through the task. Others may have been coaching another classmate. Or perhaps the students had completed the task in less time than the teacher had planned and needed a more challenging task. The teacher had used power and control to stop children from doing something that may have helped more of them in the long run. If she had instead shared power and control by listening and observing, she may have been able to see students helping each other or themselves, which could have given her time to assist a child who needed more one-on-one attention.

What you do:

- Remind yourself daily that making children be still and quiet doesn't mean they are learning. Too much quiet means that young minds are not being "exercised" enough, not stretching and growing. Muscles that are not exercised enough may atrophy. Unless your class is in the library, let children move and talk.
- Let them talk to each other because *it's good for them*. How will children who need to increase their vocabulary catch up if you don't let them talk?
- Encourage activity and spend more time observing and listening.
- Ask them what they think about what you are teaching them.

What children do:

- They have conversations at the beginning of the school year about what's important to them about learning.
- They decide what they would like to do without having to raise their hands (like sharpening their pencils).
- They behave as if they *also* are responsible for their learning.
- They began to practice leadership skills such as decision making, negotiation, and conflict resolution.

How it looks:

- Small groups of children are discussing a question you've given them based on something you've taught.
- Children spend ample time (ample means *more* than just *enough*) engaging their own learning interest.
- Children are focused because they are interested.
- You have more opportunities to observe each individual child's progress.

How it sounds:

- Children are talking and you are listening, so you can use that information to inform what you do next.
- You are not "playing teacher" by talking all the time because you think it sounds more "teacher-like."
- Children are negotiating resolutions (like whose turn it is) without having to involve you.
- It sounds a little bit noisier because children are actively engaging with what you are teaching by talking about it and doing it.

How it feels:

- You remind yourself daily that this is *their* education.
- *You* are really excited because *they* are really excited about a learning task.
- You follow their lead when they are actively engaged and let them continue to engage with the task.
- You choose not to move on to the next task on your agenda just because "it's time to move on."

How it's structured:

- You plan on having several times during the day when the children decide what to do, either individually or as a group.
- You reduce the number of paper-based activities (worksheets) to increase active engagement.
- You let children *show* you or *tell* you what they're learning.
- You embed a lot of open-ended questions both to individuals and to a group to encourage more decision making.

▶ SHARING DISCOURSE AND IDEAS

Teachers must move away from too much talking and toward more opportunities for children to do the talking. This does not mean teachers do not talk or that children talk about anything all the time. Effectiveness is somewhere in between, with a three-way conversation: teacher talks to children, children talk to teacher, and children talk to each other. For many Black children, education is about discourse and ideas. They like to talk about interesting things to see how their thinking compares to someone else's. This lets them be challenged intellectually, and the ability to challenge children intellectually is a critical ingredient that differentiates the ordinary classroom from the extraordinary one. Challenging Black children intellectually is cultivating their genius.

Sharing discourse and ideas is also about providing children with the opportunity to connect what you are teaching to what they already know. Too often teachers (at all levels) assume that learners (at all levels) know little to nothing about the topic at hand. They come to teach and teach they do. That's the "too much talking" I'm talking about. Inviting children into the conversation gives you a chance to learn more about their relationship to the topic. You may find that they know more than you think. They usually do. You may also find that they have misconceptions about the subject, which means reconsidering how you approach it.

Opening up the discourse to include children more also creates wonderful opportunities for connecting dots between what you are teaching and what children are thinking. I have always connected dots. It's one of my favorite activities. Connecting dots allows you to engage in possibility thinking and move beyond reproducing a predetermined picture, activity, or idea. It allows you to ask "what if" and expand your notions of what could be. It represents something you may not have considered before, could not have seen before, did not think was possible before. When you share the classroom discourse with children, you create space for them to connect that discourse with their own ideas—or come up with new ideas. That's what education should be about: coming up with new ideas.

What you do:

- Take advantage of the strong verbal and narrative tradition found in African-based cultures.
- Ask open-ended questions and follow-up probes most of the time.
- *Tell* children stories, don't only *read* stories.
- Encourage children to tell stories with relevant wordless picture books.

What children do:

- They have lots of who, what, when, where, why, and how conversations.
- They ask lots of questions themselves.
- They share their opinions and ideas.
- They have conversations that require judgment, inference, scientific prediction, and problem solving.

How it looks:

- You are having meaningful conversations with children.
- Children are having meaningful conversations with you.
- Children are having meaningful conversations with each other.
- Ideas, thoughts, and topics expand and grow richer and deeper as Black children's voices are included more into the classroom dialogue.

How it sounds:

- Children are talking.
- You constantly ask for their opinions and ideas.
- High-level conversations take place, *regardless of the children's ages*.
- It sounds dynamic and synergetic as the content comes to life.

How it feels:

- You feel like you are not the only one in the room who knows about the topic.
- Children feel like they know something about the topic and can contribute.
- Children feel that you value their ideas, opinions, and knowledge.
- You feel like you know and understand your individual students on a deeper level.

How it's structured:

- You always find out *from the very beginning* what students know about the subject being taught.
- You demonstrate the connections between what they know and what you are teaching.
- You give older children five minutes of "think time" before discussions instead of the normal zero to five seconds. Younger children may need less time to maintain their focus.
- You develop a rubric to ensure that every single child has multiple opportunities to engage in meaningful discourse and share his ideas daily.

▶ SHARING THE ROOM

The classroom is the children's workspace. It is where they do the most important tasks of their workday. Too often, classrooms look more like the teacher's office—filled with teacher's art, treasures, trinkets, posters, and sometimes even furniture. In many classrooms it is unclear what is learning material and what is a decoration or special item that children are not allowed to touch. Walls and bulletin boards are filled with what teachers want children to see, and there may be very little space left for children's work to be displayed.

Sharing the room means that each year the children coming into the room have some input regarding what's on the walls and bulletin boards, what cultures are represented, and even what additional learning objects and materials need to be included. Yes, there are learning centers and interest areas filled with items determined by the teacher, the curriculum, and the learning objectives, but children can tell you what they would like to have in the room, and many families are more than happy to contribute items from home that increase the cultural relevance of the learning environment.

Everything in the environment should be viewed through a teaching and learning lens. If you aren't teaching with it and children aren't actively learning from it, it probably should not be there. I have been in classrooms that are absolutely lovely—for grown-ups. One such classroom for four-year-olds had posters of scenic views from around the world, but they were above the children's eye level and the teacher never referred to them or talked about them for the whole first month I was observing. She said she didn't know what to tell the children about them or how to fit them into the curriculum—that they were mostly there because she liked to look at them. She also had a globe on her desk that children couldn't touch because they might drop it. Children did ask about the globe and other objects she had on display. She explained that they were "special" so the children could look but not touch. The room also had a lot of purple in it because that was the teacher's favorite color.

Sharing the room means not decorating every square inch before the first day of class. That makes a lot of teachers a little anxious—leaving a blank bulletin board, empty wall space, an open shelf, a blank canvas to be filled by children. Sharing the room means having a learning environment that reflects that year's children, a space they know is theirs because they see themselves reflected in it.

What you do:

- Severely limit the number of items in the room that children cannot touch.
- Leave *twice* as much space blank as you feel comfortable leaving.
- Invite children to tell you what they would like to put in those blank spaces.
- Invite families to bring culturally relevant, everyday items to the classroom.

What children do:

- They have opportunities to work with, manipulate, learn from, and investigate just about everything placed in their learning environment.
- They decide colors, themes, items, and objects for their learning environment.
- They can ask questions about and discuss anything in the room because it is tied to a learning outcome for that year.
- They bring items from home to add to the learning environment and take them back at the end of the year in order to leave space for next year's class.

How it looks:

- The room is filled with lots of interesting, challenging items and activities that represent Black culture.
- There are centers or interest areas that address Black children's learning styles and preferences.
- You see children engaged in a variety of creative activities (art, play, invention, drama, singing).
- Items in the room connect Black children to Africa and African America in the present (pictures of downtown Nairobi today, not just the Serengeti as it could have looked fifty years ago).

How it sounds:

- There is low-volume music (instrumental or drums) playing.
- Children are verbally connecting items and objects on the walls, bulletin boards, and shelves to learning objectives and their own lives and experiences.
- You are talking about, discussing, and teaching with all of the items and objects in the room.
- The conversational level will be active and excited as children spend *ample* work time engaged with the interesting, compelling, relevant materials in their learning environment.

How it feels:

- It feels like Black children are global anthropologists, not just U.S. historians. The African people are over 8,000 years old. Make sure your environment reflects this and doesn't just focus on the last 400 years in the United States.
- It feels familiar to Black children.
- It is energizing and filled with opportunities to explore and discover something new around every corner.
- It could feel a bit eclectic to teachers who have not shared the classroom with Black children this much.

How it's structured:

- Items are also labeled in African languages when there are Black children in your class. Using African languages supports home language for African children and supports second language acquisition for English-speaking Black children.
- You intentionally teach the children higher-level oral language skills.
- You try out nontraditional use of classroom space, such as having children in "pods" in the four corners of the room with your desk in the middle.
- You and the children decorate the room together, and you leave most of the space to display children's work.

▶ SHARING THE DAILY ROUTINE

The daily routine is what guides activity, action, and interaction throughout the day. It determines what children will do, where they will do it, how they will do it, with whom, and for how long. True, it provides children important structure and "patterning" that create a strong foundation for cognitive and social-emotional development, but it can also be so tightly controlled that the real objective is lost. When asked what math was, one insightful youngster said, "That's what my teacher does at 10:15." Sharing the daily routine means finding that balance between structure, opportunity, and flexibility. This balance is important because the daily routine cannot just be about a schedule of teaching activities.

It has to be about learning. My dear colleague, the late Dr. Zakiya M. Stewart, had a cartoon strip (titled *Tiger* by cartoonist Bud Blake) that she shared regularly with our teacher preparation students at PONW.

> PANEL 1: Two boys are looking at a dog and the first boy says, "I taught Stripe how to whistle."
> PANEL 2: Both boys are staring at the dog. The second boy says, "I don't hear him whistling."
> PANEL 3: The first boy responds, "I said I taught him. I didn't say he learned it."

The end result of your daily routine must be about learning, not just teaching. The daily routine is a guide that helps children move more easily through transitions and predict what will happen next during their day. Children slowly begin to understand the "pattern" of the day, the week, the month, then the year. This takes time! The three-year-olds get super excited about events like the first snowfall of the season because the last time they experienced such an event was a year ago when they were two. How would they know that 365 days later it might happen again? How would they have known at age two what 365 days even means? To many grown-ups snow is cause for worry: will I be able to drive home in it? For three-year-olds it is a miracle: will I be able to go outside and play in it?

Sharing the daily routine means taking advantage of the learning opportunities that come up at unexpected times. A teacher who has a strong sense of the learning outcomes for the year can use the snowfall to reinforce or introduce or set the stage for making connections between learning and children's lives. Once I was with a class of three-year-olds who were going to the lunchroom. Inside, most of the children were lining up to get their lunch trays, but one little boy discovered a dead spider on the windowsill. Needless to say, he excitedly announced his discovery. Also needless to say, about three other boys rushed over to have a look. They had probably been discussing and poking the spider for about thirty seconds, maybe forty-five, when the teacher came over, told them they only had twenty more minutes to eat, swooped up the spider in a napkin, and herded the very disappointed boys back into line. This was a missed anatomy and physiology lesson in much the same way a snowfall can become a missed meteorology and environmental lesson. The daily routine should not overshadow emergent learning opportunities that can be linked to learning goals and objectives that integrate children's own learning interests.

Flexibility with the daily routine is equally important. Flexibility is being so in tune with your children that you know when it may be time to "go with the flow" or "cut your losses." Going with the flow is allowing children to continue their engagement with something that has captivated their interest, be it a discussion, a task, a story, whatever. Instead of ending "because it's time," perhaps you let the learning continue for another five to ten minutes, taking advantage of their focus and persistence. On the other hand, cutting your losses is paying attention to times when children seem quite disengaged from the task at hand. Are they completely not understanding what you are expecting them to do? Have you related the task or connected it to what they already know? Is it time to move them to the next level and provide more of a challenge? Flexibility with the daily routine allows you to track learning progress throughout the day and make adjustments to the schedule as needed.

What you do:

- You make sure you are deeply and intimately familiar with the shared learning goals and objectives for the year.
- You pay attention to time, but you pay even more attention to the children.
- You take advantage of children's keen interest and find links between their interest and what you are trying to accomplish.
- You discuss the daily routine with children at the beginning of the day, throughout the day, and at the end of the day. The daily routine is an experience that teaches, not a piece of paper with times on it.

What children do:

- They review the daily routine at the beginning, throughout, and at the end of every day.
- They predict what is going to happen next and what they will be doing next.

- They become so familiar with what is expected of them that they can tell the substitute teacher how the day is organized.
- They know that if something really exciting comes up, you will weave it into their day.

How it looks:

- There is a balance of intense focus and active engagement.
- You can see that children are confident and comfortable because they know what is going to happen.
- Transitions between activities go smoothly because you extended time or reduced time as needed.
- As a result, you see children consistently engaged with the teaching and learning process throughout the day.

How it sounds:

- It sounds lively and energetic when children make a new discovery or experience a new event.
- You hear yourself speaking more with children about making adjustments to the day's schedule.
- Children sound satisfied, not frustrated.
- *You* sound satisfied, not frustrated.

How it feels:

- It feels like great things are accomplished each day.
- It feels like mutual enjoyment in being together with each other.
- It feels less stressful and rushed.
- Both you and the children feel "accomplished" because learning goals and objectives were met even if schedule times weren't strictly followed.

How it's structured:

- Know inside and out the shared learning goals, objectives, and expectations for the year.
- Make note of the variety of ways those goals, objectives, and expectations can be met.

- Review your daily routine to ensure there is enough time allowed in the important areas, such as work/play time.
- When something new emerges, make quick note of its relationship with and connection to teaching and learning. Emergent curriculum should always be clearly and intentionally linked to a learning outcome or a program goal.

▶ SHARING CLASSROOM MANAGEMENT

This one is fun. No, really. Well, fun for me anyway. I would say that in 90 percent of my work with teachers, I find they are most concerned with classroom management. It's almost as if they are going into the classroom management profession, not the teaching profession. Much like sharing power and control, sharing classroom management is unfathomable to many teachers. To some, it's tantamount to succumbing to a mutiny. In reality, sharing classroom management with children has the opposite effect. Dr. Zakiya also used to say that good classroom management is all about developing strategies that avoid or prevent misbehavior by maintaining high student interest and engagement (Stewart 2003). Children rarely misbehave or cause disruptions if they are engaged and interested, and understand expectations. You just have to keep the following in mind:

- The Big Picture
- Guiding vs. Controlling
- Teaching vs. Parenting
- Disciplining vs. Punishing

I have said it repeatedly and will repeat it again: you have to have a firm, clear, well-planned goal for the year when it comes to learning objectives, outcomes, and expectations. That's the Big Picture. Where are you and parents headed with all these young children? As a result of spending time with you, your curriculum, your program, and your school, what will children have gained, learned, become, and achieved? What will be the impact on their cognitive, social, emotional, and physical development? If you are unclear where you are headed, it is unlikely you will get there. And neither will the children. To prepare Black children (and all other children) for future leadership, you will need a classroom environment that provides them opportunities to develop leadership skills and abilities, and you need to allow them to *actually do those things*. Being still and quiet for periods of time that feel like eternity will not lead to a lot of leadership. Stillness and quiet have their place, but they should not be the goal. They should not be the Big Picture.

The first thing to do is to understand the differences between strategies that guide behavior and those that control behavior. Most children engage in specific behaviors for specific reasons. Very few behaviors are random. Even behaviors like hitting and biting are usually in response to something a child wants or needs, a "solution" to what the child considers to be a problem. You want to focus on guiding behavior, not controlling children. Telling children what they *can't* do, like having a "no hitting" rule, is an attempt to control children who hit. Telling children what they *can* do, such as having "problem-solving strategies," is a way to guide children toward a more positive reaction to a problem. Besides, it is very difficult to control another human being of any age. Once a child figures out that "no" is a response, there is no going back. Control begins to require increasingly authoritarian behavior on your part, which can become a form of oppression as your fears of losing control increase. Guiding behavior is much more freeing for all parties involved. You get to focus on the behaviors that are more productive and that allow opportunities to practice good problem-solving, conflict resolution, and decision-making skills.

Second, you need to understand how teaching strategies and parenting strategies are alike and how they are different. Both parents and the teacher may share goals, objectives, outcomes, and expectations for the child, but parents have a vested interest in the child's growth, development, and well-being for a lifetime, whereas the teacher may only be involved for a year or two. What the teacher wants for that child and how the teacher influences that child must fit within the parents' larger vision. This is why teachers who consult with parents at the beginning of the year are generally more successful with the children in their classrooms. If I want my child to be a thoughtful decision maker and his teacher just wants him to follow directions immediately, we will be working at cross-purposes in our teaching/parenting relationship and giving my child opposing messages regarding appropriate classroom behavior.

Finally, you must have a clear understanding of the differences between discipline and punishment. Discipline can consist of self-control, self-restraint, mastery, education, and collaborative effort. Punishment, on the other hand, can consist of confrontation, enforcing strict obedience, humiliation, criticism, and retribution. Which do you think young children would prefer in their teaching and learning environment? Helping children develop discipline is far more useful than punishing them for misbehavior. No, you will not suddenly have a room full of constantly darling angels who never need redirecting. We don't even get that with grown-ups in college or at work. However, when you share the development of your classroom management guidelines, many children and especially Black children will relish the opportunity to show you how they can manage themselves. And then, instead of spending time futilely trying to control children, you can focus on fruitful endeavors such as cultivating their genius.

What you do:

- You learn more about personality types/traits that are more prevalent among Black children so that you have a better idea of what you might expect to see.
- You learn more about strategies and methods regarding how to teach to different types/traits.
- You meet individually with families to discuss, compare, and contrast teaching and parenting styles, expectations, strategies, and outcomes.
- You develop classroom guidelines collaboratively with children.

What children do:

- They participate in deciding the rules of their classroom behaviors and interactions.
- They decide how they would like to resolve disagreements and conflicts with each other.
- They will reflect on (talk about and think about) situations when they have broken the rules.
- They offer options for making amends for rules they have broken.

- They will learn important skills such as restraint, self-control, and persistence.

How it looks:

- There will be pictures and examples of people of African descent (current as well as past, alive as well as deceased) around the world who are teachers, doctors, engineers, lawyers, scientists, inventors, politicians, and other such professions that give Black children a wide range of ideas about their futures.
- There are puzzles, checkers, chess, and other problem-solving games.
- Children are paying attention to the behavior expected of them and cooperating with shared goals in mind.
- Children are demonstrating skills and abilities that look remarkably like those possessed by the leaders we are preparing them to become.

How it sounds:

- Problem solving sounds more like negotiation.
- Everyone is having conversations, not arguments.
- Higher-level reasoning and critical thinking can be heard.
- What you will never hear is a child's name used as punishment (*DEBRA*!! Stop that right now!!), turning something lovingly chosen for a precious baby into an instrument of torture and humiliation.

How it feels:

- Black children feel a connection to the importance of interpersonal relationships and the communal feeling of being responsible for each other's welfare.
- Teachers feel a more meaningful relationship with the Black children in the classroom because they understand their personality types/traits and incorporate that information into the teaching and learning environment.
- Children feel their teachers understand them better.

- Teachers feel they have created shared expectations for children and a collaborative community with parents and families.

How it's structured:

- You begin the year by cocreating a larger community made up of you, the children, and their families with shared goals and expectations.
- Together, you and the children discuss how you will treat and care for each other as a community.
- When problems, conflicts, challenges, and misbehavior arise, you have a humane, skill-/ability-developing process in place for addressing them. "Zero tolerance" approaches must be used carefully. Such approaches simply become a way to avoid conversations or discussions with children and parents.
- When children are off task, you need a process whereby you can determine why they are off task (there may be good reason), whether to refocus or to redirect, to gently reengage their interest, and to remind yourself constantly not to default to controlling behaviors.

All of this sharing requires a thorough knowledge of the children in your classroom. In 2006, I went to Kenya with twelve African American educators to visit schools, preschool through university level. At the beginning of the school year, teachers in Kenya review each of their students' files. There are archive rooms where documentation of each student's academic progress is kept. I'm not talking about notes that indicate all the things the child has done wrong. I'm talking about information on where the child is academically compared to the curriculum and using it to find the child's "Zone of Proximal Development"— that place Lev Vygotsky discussed as the perfect point to take what a child does well and use that as leverage to scaffold her to the next level (Vygotsky 1978). By studying their students' files every year, Kenyan teachers know exactly what each child needs to succeed and progress to the next level.

Reflections

- Every child has both gifts and challenges. Every gifted child has challenges, and every challenging child has gifts. Describe what you know about the gifts of Black children in your classroom.

- What if you could focus *only* on Black children's gifts and not so much on their challenges?

- When you think about your classroom management strategies, what is guidance, what is discipline, and what is only punishment?

- What is your definition of power, control, and management?

- Are you anxious, nervous, or unsure about "sharing" with Black children and families? Why or why not?

- Which "share" is your easiest one? Why? How can you build on that success?

- Which "share" is your biggest challenge? Why? What will you do about that?

- Being honest with yourself, how much control do you *prefer* to have? If it's a lot, you need to know that about yourself.

- What do you know about the personality types/traits of the Black children in your classroom? How is that knowledge reflected in your classroom management?

- Describe your process for finding out what parents want for their children. How will you go about incorporating those desires into your annual plan?

- Think of the age of the children you are teaching. What is the best way to find out what they want to learn during the school year?

- You have a Black child who is struggling with a concept and you suspect he may just have a learning style that doesn't match what you are doing. How will you help create a better match?

- Take one learning objective and describe all the ways you would know that a child met that objective using every learning style and all the multiple intelligences.

- When it comes to multiple intelligences, what strategies will you use to make sure every child has a chance to shine, to make sure "every pony gets to the front of the merry-go-round"?

- Which personality type seems most opposite to yours? What strategies can you use to ensure that your management of your classroom does not unfairly penalize the type that is most unlike you?

- Write down the who, what, when, where, why, and how questions that you ask Black children during the day. What are your strategies for increasing the number and complexity of the questions?

- How can you encourage higher-level thinking and conversations for Black children?

- What items in your classroom are "not for children"? If you want to keep the items there, how can you incorporate them into the year's learning objectives?

- How would you describe your energy level? What strategies do you use to "bridge" your energy level with that of the children in your classroom?

- In what ways can you link real games to learning objectives (for example, linking Candy Land and early math concepts)?

CHAPTER 6

Changing Relationships with Black Families and Communities

It also takes a village to *educate* a child. Building strong, authentic, collaborative relationships with Black families is the key to increasing family engagement. In general, children come with grown-ups, most of whom really want academic achievement and excellence for their children, and teachers do not always get to choose which grown-up they will engage with or to decide who is family and who is not. The grown-up who is most involved in a child's education will be the most reliable source of information about the child's preferences and progress. This may not always be the mother or the father. A collaborative, communal approach to child rearing is common among many Black families. The best person to work with when it comes to a specific child's education may be Grandma or Auntie. This does not mean that Mom and Dad are not involved, but parents' work schedules may not make it feasible for all parents to be available during the teacher's work schedule. There are strong familial practices that assist Black families in sharing the work of "growing children into grown-ups." Sharing child rearing is part of the cultural capital Black families possess that supports their children's success in school and beyond.

▶ CULTURAL CAPITAL AND THE BLACK COMMUNITY

I've talked a lot about Black learning preferences and the influence of culture. Keeping in mind that all Black people are not the same and that globally people of African descent represent thousands of ethnic groups, there are still some shared historical experiences (both diasporan and continental) that have resulted in the development of cultural capital. Cultural capital comprises the tangible and intangible attitudes and knowledge needed to be successful. Understanding more about the cultural capital Black people bring to cross-cultural interactions helps you find effective ways to draw out and build on the talents, strengths, and experiences of Black people and their culture. Tara Yosso (2005) examines six forms of cultural capital (aspirational, linguistic, familial, social, navigational, and resistant); Lindsay Pérez Huber (2009) discusses spiritual capital.

Aspirational capital is maintaining future hopes and dreams in the face of both real and perceived barriers. It's a culture of possibility and resilience that can break the links between parents' current status and their children's future attainment.

Black people have always been resilient and have, as a people, maintained a belief in possibility, hopes, and dreams, despite enslavement, prejudice, racism, segregation, and other forms of oppression. Black parents have a strong belief that education is the key to liberation and advancement.

Linguistic capital includes the intellectual and social skills learned through communicating in more than one language and/or dialect. Black students often come to college with multiple language and communication skills such as a storytelling tradition, which would increase the ability to communicate with visual art, music, or poetry.

It is important to remember that enslaved Africans taught themselves how to read in a foreign language, often while hiding in a closet with a candle and a Bible, risking death or dismemberment. The African oral tradition is found easily in Black churches, spoken word, politics, music, hip-hop, and storytelling.

Familial capital describes a sense of community history, memory, and cultural intuition. It includes a commitment to community well-being and expands the concept of family kinship, incorporating extended family and ancestors.

When any people find themselves in a different culture, family and community can become a vital and crucial aspect of transition and survival. Because Africans were intentionally separated from family and language groups, extended family, "foster" family, and community collective history and experience were sometimes the only way to find a sense of belonging and create a new identity.

Social capital is made up of peer and other social contacts that can provide the instrumental and emotional supports to navigate social institutions.

People of African descent are often relational and communal. We make eye contact and acknowledge each other even if we are strangers passing on the sidewalk ("I see you."). We will often share strategies for success in unfamiliar situations, and even though we definitely do not all know one another, we will help other Black people connect with those we do know.

Navigational capital is the ability to maneuver through institutions that were not designed with Black people in mind. Navigating racially hostile college and university campuses requires students to maintain levels of achievement, despite the stressful events and conditions that may put them at risk of dropping out of school.

It is because of our aspirational capital that we have strong navigational capital. In the United States, Black people had to develop skills early on to navigate institutions (academic, medical, business, social, political) in ways that both decrease danger and increase access and, ultimately, success. The fact that Black culture continues to survive and thrive in this country is a testament, in and of itself, to Black resilience, determination, and strength.

Resistant capital describes the knowledge and skills developed through oppositional behavior when challenging inequality. It reaches fullness in the historical pattern of resistance to subordination practiced by people who have been oppressed.

People of African descent, as a whole, have always fought against enslavement, colonization, inequality, and oppression injustice—even if it meant death. Some of our country's greatest examples of activism for equity and equality have come from the Black community's refusal to accept subordination.

Spiritual capital consists of the resources and skills found in a spiritual connection to a reality or power greater than oneself. Spiritual capital includes religious, indigenous, and ancestral beliefs and practices learned from family and community, as well as inner self-spirituality, all of which support hope and faith.

Black people are a spiritual people, be that religious, indigenous, ancestral, or internal. This sense of being connected to a greater reality often merges with other important aspects of Black culture and history, such as resistance to enslavement; maintaining hopes, dreams, and will in hostile circumstances; and knowing that no one individual is in this experience alone.

Knowing more about Black cultural capital can assist teachers in developing real and collaborative relationships with Black parents and families as they work together to ensure academic success and excellence for Black children.

▶ ENGAGING BLACK PARENTS AND FAMILIES

A key first step in building authentic relationships is listening. Listen to parents. Ask questions. Do not draw your own conclusions about anything (what they want, how they feel, their home lives, their neighborhoods, their values, their experiences). Put your own preferences, values, beliefs, and perceptions on hold long enough to get real and valuable information from Black parents. And continue to remind yourself that relationships take time. You can be authentic instantly, but authentic relationships will take time—time for parents to get to know you, time for them to trust you, time for them to trust you with their child. This is true for most parents, but it is particularly true for Black parents who may have had challenging school experiences themselves. Yet even with that in mind, Black parents want their children to have the opportunity to reach their full potential, and you have a role in providing that opportunity.

Many Black parents are quite anxious about their children's education. They want their children to do well in school, but many school systems in the United States have not done well when it comes to educating

Black children. Yes, there are all the caveats noted in the introduction, but the bottom line is that the Black community produced some of our country's finest doctors, educators, lawyers, scientists, poets, engineers, writers, and activists during a time when it was illegal for us to have access to White institutions. Black parents know that high levels of academic achievement are possible—it's just a matter of learning more about the learning needs of more children. They are anxious because they want their children to do well, just like my father did for me. But the reality is that Black children spend too much time outside the classroom—sitting in the hall, in the principal's office, in special education. In many Black families, the grown-ups remember their own school experiences and have conflicting feelings. As teachers of Black children, you must take this "historical experience" into consideration when consulting with Black parents. You have daily opportunities to share with Black parents all of the genius you see in their children. No parent wants to hear a constant litany of what his child cannot do. Every parent wants to hear about the ways in which his child is excelling. Unfortunately, when learning preferences and learning environment don't mesh, children lose. Frustrated, anxious parents try to force their young children to adapt, to conform to a learning environment that doesn't work for them. Children get into trouble at school for trying to use learning approaches that make sense to them but not to the teacher, which means they also get into trouble at home. As a teacher of Black children, you are perfectly poised to allay parents' fears and anxieties by building on Black children's learning preferences and regularly communicating to parents all of the marvelous things their children can do, all of their incredible gifts and strengths. I imagine my father would have been thrilled to know that I was ahead of the reading level expected in kindergarten.

So what is culturally appropriate engagement? In Kenya, we found that the approach to parent and family engagement was very different from what we were accustomed to seeing in the United States. For one thing, there was no expectation that parents in Kenya would *volunteer* in schools. Teachers do not go to the children's homes to help parent, and parents do not go to the children's schools to help teach. Parent *involvement* in Kenya is with the child, not the school. Parent *engagement* is the relationship between the teacher and the parent and how they work together to support student learning. The teacher's role is to know where each student is academically and select appropriate learning tasks that balance work the student can successfully complete with work that challenges the student toward new learning. Parents' role is to make sure their students have time to *study*. Yes, study. Kenyan parents are not expected to *teach* in the sense of sitting with their children and doing homework with them. The student's role is to study and learn. It is generally not the case that the student is unable to do the work he has brought home. Study, practice, review, and work that provide a challenge can all take place without a parent having to sit alongside. This does not mean that parents have no role in their children's education. They do—in the form of supplementing what children are learning through home and community activities. For example, if young children are learning about colors, parents contextualize that learning by having conversations with children about colors as they go about their day. They do not go over worksheets about colors. This is an example of how experiential learning and the importance of relationship have carried over to Black people in the United States. Always remember the interpersonal. A phone call or a conversation is more interpersonal than a flyer or an email. If you send a note, address it to a specific parent or family and make it personal about a specific event.

▶ HOMEWORK

And now an aside about homework. I would say that homework, in general, can be very problematic for children, parents, and probably many teachers, regardless of race, ethnicity, economic status, you name it. Homework is the bane of most parents' evening existence. Although it doesn't show up as much with younger children, it slowly increases over the years. There are entirely too many children who have no idea how to complete the homework sent home by their teacher. Tired parents spend too much time trying to figure out what the teacher wants or explaining it like it was done "in the olden days" while frustrated children keep telling parents that's not how teacher wants it. Then the whole kit and caboodle winds up stuffed in a corner of a backpack, never to be seen again. By the time children are older, some parents just do their homework for them (can you say science project?). If you must give homework, please try a few of these suggestions:

- Send home tasks that you know the child can do alone. Children need to know they can be successful on their own in order to persist with new challenges. They should have tasks in areas of strength to build on and tasks in areas of challenge to improve.
- Try providing three to four levels of work if children are at three to four levels of learning. One level may be just the basics that you know every child has mastered. This is for the children who need to experience some successes. The next level may be the basics plus a few slightly more difficult items for students who are feeling successful and need to attempt a challenge or two for motivation. The third level may include even more challenge tasks, and the fourth may be a balance of opportunities for success and for challenge.
- Children should not have more than twenty to thirty minutes of "sit down and work alone" homework per night. Young ones should have even less. I'm not talking about the time parents may spend reading to or with children. Reading together is a social activity that can take place in the evening on the couch with a book or on Saturday at the grocery store reading signage and packaging.
- Homework should count for only a small percentage, maybe 10 percent, of a child's overall classroom grade. You should know more about a child's academic progress from what you observe, hear, and experience for hours in the classroom than from tasks sent home to be completed in a few minutes.
- Encourage children to *study*. Studying is going back over what you have learned, reviewing what you did in class, even telling someone what you are learning in school. I believe studying is much more productive than homework. My children were always so focused on trying to complete homework that the idea of just studying was an alien notion. Parents can support studying anywhere anytime.
- Parents should know what the learning objective is each week *in advance*. If you have consulted with parents in the beginning of the year, they should know what you plan to

teach and when. If I know my child is learning about colors this week, I can be intentional about talking about colors all week—in the store, running errands, cooking dinner, anytime. This is how I can help my child study. Teachers can assist by regularly giving parents a schedule of weekly learning objectives that includes ideas for building on those objectives through regular, daily, at-home activities.

- Link homework with what parents want their children to learn. Consultations with parents at the beginning of the year will ensure that you know their goals for their children.

Reflections

- What do you know about the aspirations Black families have for their children? What are the aspirations of the Black community? How did you learn this?

- What are the languages and dialects of the Black families you serve? How do you build on Black linguistic strengths?

- Describe what you know about Black values and priorities regarding family and parenting. What aspects of your program encourage the familial strengths of your Black families and the Black community?

- What are the steps/actions you can take to strengthen your connection and children's social connections to extended family and community? How can you learn more about children's current social connections?

- What practices need to be in place to assist Black families and the Black community in navigating your program and institutions? What barriers and challenges does your program or institution have that may strain relationships with Black families or the Black community?

Academic achievement through homework can work as long as Black learning preferences are incorporated from the beginning. The current format for most homework almost completely eliminates cultural preferences for experiential and contextualized learning, collaboration between parents and teachers, and positive interactions between parents and their children.

Engaging Black families is all about incorporating many of the cultural and learning preferences discussed in this book regarding Black children. It all about valuing Black culture, understanding Black cultural capital, and increasing your knowledge of the learning styles,

- What do you know about the barriers and challenges your Black families face in your community? How do you support Black advocacy efforts and initiatives?

- In what ways do you connect children with each other for their own well-being and the good of the whole?

- In what ways do you connect Black children's community strengths to what they are learning in class? How are Black children in your classroom beginning to see themselves as a global people?

- As with children, grown-ups also have gifts and challenges. Describe the gifts of the Black parents whose children are in your classroom.

- Describe the ways you incorporate interpersonal, relationship-based communications with Black parents.

- What are some of your strategies for working more with Black parents and learning more about the Black community?

multiple intelligences, and personality types/traits that are more dominant among people of African descent. In the next chapter, you will have the opportunity to follow one young teacher's intentional and reflective journey and what change and redirection look like as she transforms her classroom in order to cultivate the genius of Black children one step at a time.

CHAPTER 7

Story Time: One Teacher's Journey

ORGAN WAS EXCITED. She had just been offered a position as a lead teacher in a pre-K classroom in Seattle. The meeting that August with the program director was very useful as she prepared to start the new school year. It turned out that almost 75 percent of the children she would be teaching represented non-European ethnic and racial groups. The incoming class for Morgan included children of African, Asian, Latino, and European descent and represented twelve different ethnic groups with almost the same number of language groups. This was a big change from Eugene, Oregon, where she had grown up and where over 85 percent of the children in her previous classroom were of European descent. At first, thinking about how to meet the learning needs of such a diverse classroom was a bit overwhelming for Morgan, even though she had studied learning styles, multiple intelligences, and personality types/traits in her early childhood education teacher preparation program.

In her previous classroom, the children were not very diverse in terms of race and language, even though they had been diverse in other ways, such as their physical and cognitive abilities and their families' economic status and religion. Morgan found that, in general, she had not really had to incorporate all of the learning preferences presented to her in college. She was fairly skilled at incorporating a few that were more familiar to her, and these were her "go to" approaches. How could she fit in more? Then she remembered attending a conference presentation about moving from "scarcity thinking" toward "abundance thinking."

In scarcity thinking, only so many learning preferences fit in a learning environment; adding more means removing others. In abundance thinking, more learning preferences can always be added to a learning environment; they just have to be added gradually in order to create a good balance. However, Morgan still didn't know how she was going to provide "abundance" for so many different children. Then she read this book about cultivating the genius of Black children. The book talked about starting with just one culture at a time. Incorporating one culture seemed much more doable than incorporating twelve, so Morgan decided to give it a try. She was going to review what she had learned in her teacher preparation program and incorporate the learning styles, multiple intelligences, and personality types/traits that were more prevalent in the Black population. According to the book, this would mean thinking about:

- sharing goals and expectations
- sharing power and control
- sharing discourse and ideas
- sharing the room
- sharing the daily routine
- sharing classroom management
- cultural capital and the Black community
- engaging Black parents and families
- homework
- active, engaged, synergetic learning environments
- interactive discourse, discussion, and analysis with an emphasis on verbal "play"
- opportunities for creativity, individualism, and embellishment
- collective/collaborative activity and problem solving
- competitive mental and physical challenges
- meaningful, mutually respectful teacher-child relationships
- meaningful, mutually respectful connection to family and community
- educational empowerment/personal responsibility
- opportunities for self-reflection
- opportunities for connecting with nature and each other for a higher purpose, good cause
- an integrated, connected curriculum
- a sense of community and belonging

A long list, yes, but Morgan knew she only had to take one step at a time.

SHARING GOALS AND EXPECTATIONS

Morgan's first step was to arrange consultations with each of her students' families in order to learn what parents' goals and expectations were. She realized that while she had her own goals and expectations, she had not consulted with her students' first teachers, their parents. At first, Morgan planned to create a rubric of her annual curriculum—including goals and objectives—and then share it with parents for their input and ideas. This seemed fairly straightforward until she considered that she was structuring the process in a way that restricted dialogue to what she was presenting. This wouldn't leave "space" for Black parents to freely and openly tell her about their children. Instead, Morgan arranged for unstructured home visits as a way to get to know more about the children as *children*, not just students. It turned out to be so much fun visiting with children and parents in their home. One young boy, Aaron, even invited his cousin over to meet his new teacher—he was that excited! This was a great start to some new relationships. Knowing more about Aaron gave Morgan fresh eyes when she did finally create her rubric to share with parents just before school began. When Aaron and his parents began listing what they wanted to have happen for the year, Morgan could already begin to see areas where she knew he would shine.

SHARING POWER AND CONTROL

Morgan knew this would be one of the more challenging elements to implement because she imagined that the classroom would be chaotic with children wandering around all over the place and talking all the time. Still, she was determined to give it a try. Her first step was to ask her students what they wished they could do without asking for her permission. There were a few far-fetched responses, like bringing a younger sibling to class, but there were also some that she knew made sense, like getting a tissue. Morgan realized she just needed to create some guidelines to feel more comfortable. Together, the children and Morgan decided that instead of one tissue box on the teacher's desk, there should be tissue boxes in other areas of the room. That way, they wouldn't have to walk across the whole room. The children also agreed that they would walk quietly to get tissues and not bother anyone else on the way. Aaron said he really liked this idea because he had noticed that grown-ups never raised their hand to get permission to get tissues. Besides, sometimes his legs just "needed a walk." He promised not to get tissues all day long, but he was glad he could stand up when he felt a little fidgety.

Another way Morgan decided to share power and control was to add a fifteen-minute "you tell me" session two days each week. Each child had a turn during the year to decide what the class would do for those fifteen minutes. Aaron's dad played congas, so he chose drumming for his session.

▶ SHARING DISCOURSE AND IDEAS

Although Morgan was still a little stuck on the notion of teaching as talking, she also knew that children really did need to talk more to increase the complexity of their sentences as well as their ideas. She decided to ask every child what he knew about a topic every time she introduced one. She was a little concerned that this would add up to a lot of time over the long run, but she wanted to see if it would really change how she approached a topic. The first topic for this experiment was about seeds and growing plants, so she asked her class what they knew about those two things. She was actually surprised that, collectively, the children knew quite a bit:

- Some seeds are big and some are little.
- Different seeds grow different kinds of food.
- Some seeds are shaped like footballs and others are shaped like tennis balls.

There was also some disagreement and confusion:

- I don't know what a kiwi is, but I don't think you should eat the seeds.
- My mom grows some flowers that come from big things that look like brown carrots, not seeds.
- Apples have seeds, but they grow from flowers on trees.

All these thoughts and ideas helped Morgan revise her lesson plan so she could weave in the children's questions, thoughts, misconceptions, and opportunities to investigate further.

▶ SHARING THE ROOM

Morgan had always wanted to teach young children. The thought of seeing their smiling, excited faces as they walked into the beautiful space she had created for them made her so happy. Recalling more of what she had read in the book about the genius of Black children, she thought to herself, "Yes, Dr. Sullivan, it is their work space, but I am in this room all day as well." During the week before the school year began, all the other teachers were busily decorating their rooms, but Morgan reluctantly decided that she would leave the bottom half of each wall completely blank. The top half would be posters that were important to her, but she made a commitment to make sure they were woven into the curriculum in some way. She had five walls in her classroom due to an awkwardly shaped corner, so a lot of blank space was left over. Some of her colleagues voiced their concern about her choice, and one even hinted that maybe she was just lazy, but Morgan went with it. After all, if she really didn't like it, she could always redecorate over the December break.

When school started, Morgan had the children divide into groups of four. She let go of a little control and let them choose their own groups; then she let each group choose a wall and decide what to do with it. Aaron and three other boys chose the awkward corner with the two smaller walls and decided to put magazine and newspaper pictures of cars they liked. The three other walls were equally eclectic. One group decided it would be their art gallery where they could put up and take down their artwork the whole year. Another group created a "photo album" by bringing in pictures of their families, friends, and pets. The last group decided they could each put up whatever they wanted, so their wall was a mix of classwork, artwork, pictures, even stickers. It wasn't the room Morgan had in mind, but the children were so engaged with their walls that she left the room that way the whole year and found interesting ways to integrate her top halves and their bottom halves into the learning content on a regular basis.

SHARING THE DAILY ROUTINE

On the Wednesday before Thanksgiving, Morgan was teaching a segment on measurement. She noticed that some of the children were paying attention, a few were trying to, but others just seemed distracted and disengaged. She was a little annoyed, but remembered that everyone was heading into a lovely four-day weekend and even *she* kept finding herself mentally running through a grocery list to be sure she hadn't forgotten anything she needed to buy. There were ten minutes left in her lesson, and her choices were either to remind the children they should be paying attention or to do something else. She kind of knew that if she continued, it was almost guaranteed that most of the segment would have to be retaught the next week, so she tossed the schedule out the window (figuratively, not literally) and asked the children what they were thinking about. Sure enough, most of them were thinking about Thanksgiving dinner and seeing cousins and friends. She asked what they liked to eat on Thanksgiving and got a variety of responses: turkey, gravy, mashed potatoes, greens, honey-glazed ham, lumpia, roasted pig, cranberry sauce, roasted chestnuts, sweet potato pie, mocha cake, green bean casserole, game hens, macaroni and cheese, salmon, pumpkin flan, injera with lentils, cornbread dressing, and so many others. She learned a lot about the different cultural traditions and was surprised that the Black children represented three different "traditional" menus. As Morgan wrote the list on the board, she thought of a way to combine it with the measurement lesson she had discarded. She had been talking about length, so she asked the children to put the list in order from shortest to longest food. There was a lot of debate regarding what size the pan might be, should macaroni be a dish or just one piece, and what about lining up the green beans in a row, but in the end they all agreed that the roasted pig was probably the longest and the chestnuts were the shortest.

SHARING CLASSROOM MANAGEMENT

Early on in her teacher preparation program, Morgan had decided to try taking a different approach to classroom management. Even while studying the topic in her teacher preparation program, she realized that she didn't really know enough about how children were expected to behave in other cultures. This was going to be important for her, because she already knew she wanted to move to Seattle someday, where her classroom was likely to be far more diverse than her classroom in Eugene. Morgan also knew that she tended to try to control children too much and that she didn't really know if she understood the distinction between discipline and punishment. She knew that one sounded better, but what would that look like in action?

During one of her first staff meetings in Seattle, Morgan asked if she and her new colleagues could discuss the differences between discipline and punishment at a staff meeting. The first thing she noticed was that there were a lot of "No" rules: No running, No talking, No touching, and on and on and on. In her classroom, she asked the children to come up with their own plans for how they would behave. In particular, she wanted to involve the four Black boys in the conversation, because she knew that having strict, controlling rules could mean they might end up being overdisciplined. It really surprised Morgan that her Black male students came up with so many positive ways to treat each other: always use your inside voice, ask permission to use something if someone else has it, get the teacher if you can't agree, and respect each other's names and bodies. And because her class was allowed to do some things without asking, she found that all of her boys, including the Black ones, were a lot less likely to be in trouble for not sitting still.

▶ CULTURAL CAPITAL AND ENGAGING BLACK PARENTS AND COMMUNITIES

During her teacher preparation program, the more Morgan read of Dr. Sullivan's *Cultivating the Genius of Black Children*, the more she realized she didn't really know anything about cultural capital, and very little about other cultures in general. There was almost no racial or ethnic diversity where she grew up, and she admitted, only to herself, that what she did know about other groups she learned from TV, movies, and the opinions of her friends and family. She had no knowledge of Black cultural capital, let alone Black culture, and she had felt awkward about taking a Black studies course or asking the African American student who sat next to her in one of their college classes. Dr. Sullivan included a number of good resources, books, and research in the book, so Morgan decided to start there. She began reading and reading and reading. Each thing she read led to another source of information, and eventually, Morgan found herself increasingly familiar with critical aspects of African and African American history and culture.

When she arrived in Seattle for her new position, Morgan felt she finally had more facts than assumptions regarding Black families and the Black community. It certainly made her feel more comfortable doing the home visits she had planned. Then she fell into the pitfall that Dr. Sullivan had warned her about. When she was meeting with Aaron and his family, they asked her about her name and if she were Irish. She confirmed that her family was Irish, but that she didn't really know much about Irish culture, history, or the experiences of Irish people in the United States. She had not really thought much about it. Aaron's parents explained to her that they appreciated sharing their culture with her, but that sharing usually went two ways. Morgan began learning more about her own culture, and as she met with her class's parents and families throughout the year, she was able to contribute more and more to the cultural conversation. This also helped her learn more about the other cultures represented in her classroom. She reread chapter 3 in Dr. Sullivan's book and developed a list of questions based on the deep culture and unconscious culture levels of the Iceberg Model (Hall 1976) using her own culture for the sample responses. Then, when families completed the form, they learned as much about her as she learned about them.

▶ HOMEWORK

Knowing more about her students and their families gave Morgan the courage to eliminate homework altogether. Her parents and families already had her learning goals and expectations for the year and she had theirs, so instead, she put together a combined list of shared learning goals, expectations, and objectives and then provided lots of examples of everyday ways parents and families could reinforce them. Parents added their own ideas to the list, and soon there was a broad variety of things to do in the car, on the bus, when walking the dog, cleaning the house, making a snack, going to birthday parties, and playing games indoors or outside. Morgan also helped the children learn how to study and provided specific ways to guide them in studying on their own. She found that she could learn a lot about how the children were meeting targets simply by observing them and listening to them talk both in school and outside school (home visits and seeing the children in other settings). Parents were thankful that the dreaded homework monster had been exiled. They found the study approach to be much better for their relationships with their children and felt validated in their involvement in their children's education through everyday living.

▶ APPROPRIATE LEARNING ENVIRONMENTS FOR CHILDREN OF AFRICAN DESCENT

At first, Morgan found the list of twelve elements for creating a learning environment that was more effective for her children of African descent a little daunting. There were pages and pages of ideas! Then she remembered that the whole point of Dr. Sullivan's book was to implement strategies *gradually*, not all at once. Morgan decided she would do one small change at a time over the course of the year.

Active, Engaged, Synergetic Learning Environment

Morgan decided that the work time in the daily schedule needed to be an hour, but she had difficulty making it fit. Instead she created two thirty-minute blocks, one in the morning and one in the afternoon. She was amazed at how quickly the children reengaged with their morning projects and activities.

Interactive Discourse, Discussion, and Analysis with an Emphasis on Verbal "Play"

Because she loved Dr. Seuss, Morgan read the Dr. Seuss books with the most outrageous "words" and wordplay. Her favorites were *There's a Wocket in My Pocket!* and *Fox in Socks*. She then had the children discuss the new "words," and she found that the Black children really loved trying to repeat phrases from *Fox in Socks* as quickly as possible.

Collective/Collaborative Activity and Problem Solving

This one was easier for Morgan because the children came up with their own ways to solve their disputes at the beginning of the year when they created their classroom guidelines. Her biggest challenge was to let the children actually engage in the process when they had disagreements, but fortunately, part of the process was that the children could remind her that they had to do it themselves unless they asked for her help.

Competitive Mental and Physical Challenges

First, Morgan got the school to buy "wobble" stools for her pre-K classroom. This made it possible for the boys (and some of the girls) to wiggle in place. It also became a great way to practice balancing skills. For the mental challenge, she made tangram shapes and scheduled regular team "design" competitions. To keep her four-year-olds mentally on their toes, Morgan also added a weekly "wordplay" time to encourage creative use of language.

Meaningful, Mutually Respectful Teacher-Child Relationship

The home visits really helped her get to know each child individually, but Morgan also spent some time learning more about personality types/traits so she could have a better sense of her own personality and how she interacted with the personalities of individual children. In the process, she also learned a lot about the personalities of her colleagues and how to respond better to them as well.

Meaningful, Mutually Respectful Connection to Family and Community

Through her home visits and cultural studies, Morgan discovered that many of the Black families had really exciting contributions to make based on their hobbies, and every day new items arrived from quilters, gardeners, carpenters, bakers, mechanics, and artists. She asked them to send in age-appropriate items to include in the classroom.

Educational Empowerment/Personal Responsibility

Because she had two thirty-minute work times during the day, Morgan used the first ten minutes of the morning session for the children to have planning time. She continued to be amazed at how focused and engaged they were when they had lots of time to follow their own interests.

Opportunities for Self-Reflection

Every Friday at the end of the day, Morgan had the children spend ten minutes or so thinking about their activities, their learning, and their goals for themselves. She wrote down what they said as a way to track how they were responding to her teaching. She was pleased when they indicated that a favorite activity was something she had taught them or wanted them to learn. She used what she discovered from their reflections to make adjustments the following week.

Opportunities for Connecting with Nature and Each Other for a Higher Purpose or a Good Cause

The Thanksgiving Day meal activity that emerged on the Wednesday before the holiday also provided opportunities for follow-up learning. When the children returned the following Monday, Morgan began a conversation about how we get our food. Everything was fine until the children began asking about the meat. Some of the children made strong connections to the animal world and said they would never eat meat again. Naturally, this entailed some follow-up conversations with parents.

An Integrated, Connected Curriculum

Once again, Morgan found that the home visits at the beginning of the year were helping in multiple ways. It was so much easier to connect the curriculum with her children's life experiences because she knew them, their families, and their communities so much better. And with the shared goals and expectations in place for Morgan, the children, and their parents, the curriculum seemed completed, connected, and related.

A Sense of Community and Belonging

Morgan liked the suggestion to create a schedule to ensure that she had a positive interaction with every child in her class every week. She noticed that a couple of the children were very quiet and easily lost among the more exuberant, talkative children. The schedule helped her remember to observe them during the day and make sure they were interacting with other children and she was interacting with them. With a schedule, she didn't have to guess.

Opportunities for Creativity, Individualism, and Embellishment

At the beginning of the school year, Morgan started "Our Story." She started with "Once upon a time . . ." and asked Aaron to finish the sentence. His response was, "There was a giraffe in my backyard." Each day after that, a new student got to make up the next sentence. By the end of the year, the class had created a unique story that didn't always make sense, but did include everyone's ideas.

The End.

CHAPTER 8

Working within Existing Models

MANY TEACHERS MAY ALREADY BE WORKING with a particular curriculum model and may be wondering how to incorporate the elements in this book. In this chapter, I'll provide an overview of how five current curriculum models already address and promote many of the elements needed to cultivate the genius of Black children. This is important to keep in mind, because sometimes teachers may feel like it's too overwhelming to try to add another layer to what they are already doing. In addition, not all teachers can easily see how certain models have embedded features that inherently support Black learning preferences. Also, unfortunately, there are some who are unsure that particular models are effective with Black learners. One teacher told me that HighScope wasn't effective with Black children from low-income communities. Of course, I had to point out that HighScope was first implemented with that exact population and that the HighScope Foundation had over forty years of data documenting its success (Schweinhart et al. 2005).[1] The Montessori Method began with poor children. The Reggio Emilia approach began after a world war. Many wonderful curriculum models were created because there were groups of children facing challenges. Today in the United States many of those same curriculum models are perceived as ineffective for children facing challenges. So, I am going to demonstrate how Black children benefit from the following models, listed in alphabetical order:

---

[1] The HighScope Foundation is currently collecting data from the participants, who are now turning fifty years old. The study is titled "Lifetime Effects: The HighScope Perry Preschool Study through Age 50."

- Creative Curriculum
- experiential learning
- HighScope
- Montessori
- Reggio-inspired approach

These five models were selected because of their widespread use in the Seattle area and the numerous ways they include elements of appropriate learning environments for Black children. I'm sure there are many others, but space and time prohibit me from including them all.

▶ CREATIVE CURRICULUM

Key Features

- Teachers use a wide variety of instructional strategies and materials.
- Whole-group, small-group, and individual instruction are part of the routine.
- The program takes into account the social/emotional, physical, cognitive, and language development of children.
- It creates a responsive environment that addresses the developing abilities and interests of children.
- It focuses on building partnerships with families—working with them as partners in the care of their children.
- It provides many and varied experiences for children.
- The schedule allows children time to practice new skills.
- Teachers develop positive relationships with each child.
- The program provides many rich language experiences throughout the day by describing what is happening, asking questions, singing, and reading.
- Each classroom is set up for exploration and learning.
- Children have many opportunities to make choices, experiment, and interact with others.
- Each child can be proactive in his or her learning.

- Materials are on low shelves, in containers, and on hooks so children can get them independently and put them away.
- Picture and word labels are on containers and shelves so children know where materials belong and learn to use print.
- Distinct interest areas and different outdoor play spaces are set up so children know what choices are available and can make decisions.
- A variety of learning materials is in each area.

Benefits for Black Children

- multiple learning styles
- multiple intelligences
- differentiated instruction throughout the day
- holistic view of Black children
- children follow own interests
- time to try out own ideas
- positive interactions with families and the Black community
- opportunities to make many choices
- time to plan their own learning
- opportunities to choose what to learn
- ample time to "work" (play)
- engagement in creative problem-solving
- interaction with the world, not just observation
- opportunities to discuss with others
- increased decision-making skills
- lots of opportunities for talking and increasing verbal skills
- increased self-control, responsibility
- ample opportunities to move around
- increased confidence, competence
- opportunities to incorporate African languages
- movement around the learning environment
- independent action and responsibility
- stimulus variety
- ample time outdoors

▶ EXPERIENTIAL LEARNING

Key Features

- Education is the realization of one's full potential, not the acquisition of a predetermined set of skills.
- Education and learning are social and interactive processes.
- Children are personally involved in the learning experience.
- Discovery is used to make meaning significant.
- Children are free to set their own learning objectives and are able to actively pursue them.
- Experiences are carefully chosen and supported by reflection, critical analysis, and synthesis.
- Children take initiative, make decisions, and are accountable for results.
- Children are actively engaged in posing questions, investigating, experimenting, being curious, problem solving, assuming responsibility, being creative, and constructing meaning.
- Children are engaged intellectually, emotionally, socially, spiritually, and/or physically.
- Learning tasks are authentic.
- The results of the learning are personal.
- Relationships are developed and nurtured: student to self, student to others, and student to the world at large.
- Students and instructors explore and examine their own values.
- Teachers set suitable experiences and pose problems.
- The approach encourages spontaneous opportunities for learning.
- Teachers strive to be aware of their biases, judgments, and preconceptions, and how these influence individual students.
- Curriculum includes the possibility to learn from natural consequences, mistakes, and successes.
- Teachers must be willing to accept a less teacher-centric role in the classroom.
- The approach facilitates the identification of experiences that will interest students.

- The purpose of the experiential learning situation is explained to students.
- Teachers share their feelings and thoughts with students and let them know that they are learning from the experience too.
- Reflection on learning during and after experiences is an integral component of the learning process.

Benefits for Black Children

- opportunities to reach their full potential
- open interactions with adults and peers
- opportunities to make many choices
- time to plan their own learning
- opportunities to choose what to learn
- engagement in creative problem solving
- ample time to "work" (play)
- time to try out own ideas
- time to follow own interests
- active, engaged learning
- opportunities for critical thinking
- opportunities for critical reasoning
- opportunities for critical analysis
- increased decision-making skills
- holistic approach to child development
- increased self-control, responsibility
- emphasized need for "realism"
- increased responsibility for learning
- engagement with each other, peer learning, and tutoring
- interaction with world, not just observation
- multiple learning styles
- multiple intelligences
- opportunities for discussions with teachers
- ample opportunities to move around
- increased confidence, competence
- child-centered, not teacher-centric, classroom
- shared power and control with teachers

- opportunities to get to know teachers
- time for children's daily reflection on their learning

▶ HIGHSCOPE

Key Features

- HighScope promotes active, participatory learning, not just listening.
- Children plan what they want to learn, have ample time to act on their plans, and then determine how things went (Plan-Do-Review).
- HighScope promotes supportive interactions with children.
- Children solve their own problems.
- Children resolve their own conflicts.
- Children make many choices.
- Children make many decisions.
- The classroom is the children's, not the teacher's.
- Daily routine reflects childrens' needs.
- Teachers rely on individualized assessment.
- Teachers keep daily individualized anecdotal notes.
- The focus is on student strengths.
- Adults and children share problem solving.
- Teachers ensure that interesting materials/objects are available.
- Teachers support children's initiative.
- HighScope uses daily team lesson planning.
- Lesson planning is based on assessment.
- Teachers complete detailed family report forms.
- Children and teachers share classroom control.
- The child's perspective is valued.

Benefits for Black Children

- open interactions with adults and peers
- opportunities to make many choices
- time to plan their own learning
- opportunities to update their plans

- opportunities to choose what to learn
- ample time to "work" (play)
- daily reflections on their learning
- increased responsibility for learning
- engagement in creative problem solving
- interaction with the world, not just observation
- multiple learning styles
- multiple intelligences
- assessment-based lesson planning
- lots of children's work displayed
- no teacher decorations, art, displays
- opportunities to discuss with others
- meaningful, intentional activities for the following day based on the children's most current interests
- increased decision-making skills
- opportunities for critical thinking
- opportunities for critical reasoning
- opportunities for critical analysis
- increased self-control, responsibility
- time to try out own ideas
- time to follow own interests
- ample opportunities to move around
- increased confidence, competence

▶ MONTESSORI

Key Features

- Children are born to learn.
- Children are thinking beings. But what they learn depends greatly on their teachers, experiences, and environments.
- Learning happens through discovery.
- Knowledge is constructed using concrete material before moving to the abstract.
- Multi-age classes consist of four-year-olds and five-year-olds.
- Individual and small-group instruction is given on individual levels.

- Self-correcting materials allow children to experience success while learning new tasks.
- Children do things and learn for themselves.
- Children have choices so they can develop the skills and abilities necessary for effective learning, autonomy, and positive self-esteem.
- Children learn from their environment.
- Classrooms are child-centered with active learning.
- Freedom is an essential characteristic.
- Children are free to explore materials of their own choosing.
- Environments should enable independent, active learning.
- According to Maria Montessori, children are capable of educating themselves when they are actively involved in an environment with freedom of choice.

Benefits for Black Children

- time to try out own ideas
- time to follow own interests
- sense of realism
- family, communal practices reflected in multi-age classrooms
- opportunities to persist
- open interactions with adults and peers
- opportunities to make many choices
- time to plan their own learning
- opportunities to update their plans
- opportunities to choose what to learn
- ample time to "work" (play)
- sharing of power and control with teachers
- increased responsibility for learning
- engagement in creative problem solving
- interaction with the world, not just observation
- multiple learning styles
- multiple intelligences
- opportunities to discuss with others
- increased decision-making skills

- opportunities for critical thinking
- opportunities for critical reasoning
- opportunities for critical analysis
- increased self-control, responsibility
- ample opportunities to move around
- increased confidence, competence

▶ REGGIO-INSPIRED APPROACH

Key Features

- Children have some control over the direction of their learning.
- Children learn through experiences of touching, moving, listening, seeing, and hearing.
- Children have relationships with other children and with material items in the world that children must be allowed to explore.
- Children must have endless ways and opportunities to express themselves.
- The approach embraces the whole child and her or his family.
- The approach welcomes and plans for parent participation.
- The approach is child-centered, teacher guided.
- Children and teachers as co-researchers.
- Learning within relationships with peers and teachers is fostered.
- The environment is considered a third teacher.
- Planned provocations provoke critical thinking and planning.
- Carefully prepared environments foster a sense of culture / ethnic belonging.
- Intentional cycles of "listen / observe, make meaning, plan" inform the daily life of the classroom, assessment, and the professional development of teachers.
- Minimum time is spent on teacher-directed activities; a maximum amount of time is given to children's investigations and creativity (play / work time).
- Daily meetings are a time when community news is reported (weather, birthdays), work is summarized, and planning takes place.

- Teacher observations (written, recorded, sketched) and children's work products drive what happens in the classroom.
- Teachers recognize the emergence of a possible project/study and nudge and scaffold a deep investigation (in-depth study) that may endure for several days, weeks, or months.
- Documentation panels make meaning visible—to the children, teachers, families, and community members.

Benefits for Black Children

- children's ownership and control of education for themselves
- movement in the classroom
- a view of the child as powerful, competent, and valued, countering negative images of Black people in society
- the whole child (cultural learning style, particular intelligences, languages spoken, interests, and passions) welcomed and valued; informs what happens in the classroom
- contributions of family members valued
- deep respect from teachers for children's ideas and efforts (children see their work recorded on documentation panel and their hypotheses and discoveries informing class planning)
- opportunities for children to connect with nature
- nurturing and celebration of differences among children and families
- frequent modification of the learning environment to support and scaffold children's current interests (rich and varied learning environment)
- large chunks of time for exploration, discovery, and creativity
- communal classroom
- teacher and parent interests reflected in the life of the classroom by honoring cultural heroines and heroes, learning relevant history (histories of resilience and resistance), experiencing cultural arts, and participating in community cultural events
- opportunities for creative expression throughout

As you can see, many of the curriculum models in use today contain elements and features that align quite well with the elements of appropriate learning environments for children of African descent. Teachers just need to be intentional about brushing aside assumptions that Black children need a completely different model. Research shows that many Black children would benefit greatly from the opportunity to participate in one of these five curriculum models, as have so many other children. Closing the academic achievement gap and cultivating the genius of Black children can happen simultaneously in classrooms that already exist.

Closing Thoughts

I REALLY ENJOYED WRITING THIS BOOK. I've been thinking about it for *years* as I've worked with, coached, mentored, and taught classroom teachers. As I said at the beginning, it can be a challenge to try incorporating a multitude of learning needs into a classroom all at one time, and I hope this book has provided you with a foundation to begin with just one. Not only will you make more learning more accessible to more Black children, you will also be providing more options and opportunities for all children in your classroom. Your work to learn more about increasing your effectiveness with Black children can serve as a template for increasing your effectiveness with all populations of children—one group at a time.

The research presented in this book is just a beginning, but do begin. The more you learn, the more you'll know. This may seem obvious, but there is so much more to learn about Black children, their families, and their communities than can be covered in a teacher preparation program—although I do think such programs could include *much* more than they do currently. You have the opportunity and the ability to learn as much as you want about Black children and their learning preferences, focusing on how making even small changes can result in big impact.

Just as learning happens one step at a time, so does change. Give yourself a year (like Morgan did) and continually reflect on how it's going. Cultivating the genius of Black children is possible, doable, and imperative. I truly believe we can eliminate the academic achievement gap many Black children face, especially in our larger, urban schools. To do so, however, we have to do something *different*. We will never be successful doing what we have done for hundreds of years that hasn't worked out for generations of Black children. Genius is a terrible thing to waste, but a glorious thing to cultivate!

Resources

BIBLIOGRAPHY

Akbar, Na'im. 1976. "Rhythmic Patterns in African Personality." In *African Philosophy: Assumption & Paradigms for Research on Black Persons*, edited by Lewis M. King, Vernon J. Dixon, and Wade W. Nobles, 175–89. Los Angeles: Fanon Center.

Armstrong, Thomas. 1994. *Multiple Intelligences in the Classroom*. Alexandria, VA: ASCD.

Ang, Soon, and Linn Van Dyne. 2008. *Handbook of Cultural Intelligence*. Armonk, NY: M. E. Sharpe.

Belgrave, Faye Z., and Kevin W. Allison. 2006. *African American Psychology: From Africa to America*. Thousand Oaks, CA: Sage.

Berger, Joseph. 1988. "Education: What Do They Mean by 'Black Learning Style'?" *New York Times*, July 6. www.nytimes.com/1988/07/06/us/education-what-do-they-mean-by-black-learning-style.html.

Blake, Bud. *Tiger*. Distributed by King Features Syndicate. Accessed May 5, 2015. www.stevemargetts.co.uk/assessment-for-learning.

Boykin, Alfred Wade. 1983. "The Academic Performance of Afro-American Children." In *Achievement and Achievement Motives*, edited by Janet Spence, 321–71. San Francisco: W. H. Freeman.

Boykin, Alfred Wade, and Caryn T. Bailey. 2000. *The Role of Cultural Factors in School Relevant Cognitive Functioning: Description of Home Environmental Factors, Cultural Orientations, and Learning Preferences* (Report No. 43). Washington, DC: Center for Research on the Education of Students Placed At Risk (CRESPAR).

Bryk, Anthony, Valerie Lee, and Peter B. Holland. 1993. *Catholic Schools and the Common Good*. Cambridge, MA: Harvard University Press.

Calahan, Margaret, and Laura Perna. 2015. *Indicators of Higher Education in the United States: 45 Year Trend Report 2015*. Washington, DC: Pell Institute for the Study of Opportunity in Higher Education.

CARLA (Center for Advanced Research on Language Acquisition). 2014. "What Is Culture?" May 27. www.carla.umn.edu/culture/definitions.html.

Curenton, Stephanie M. 2004. "The Association between Narratives and Theory of Mind for Low-Income Preschoolers." *Early Education and Development* 15 (2): 121–45.

Curenton, Stephanie M. 2011. "Understanding the Landscapes of Stories: The Association between Preschoolers' Narrative Comprehension and Production Skills and Cognitive Abilities." *Early Child Development and Care* 181 (6): 791–808.

Curenton, Stephanie M., and Iheoma Iruka. 2013. *Cultural Competence in Early Childhood Education.* San Diego: Bridgepoint.

Curenton, Stephanie M., and Laura Justice. 2004. "African American and Caucasian Preschoolers' Use of Decontextualized Language: Literate Language Features in Oral Narratives." *Language, Speech, and Hearing Services in the Schools* 35 (3): 240–53.

Delpit, Lisa. 2006. *Other People's Children: Cultural Conflict in the Classroom.* New York: New Press.

Digman, John. 1990. "Personality Structure: Emergence of the Five-Factor Model." *Annual Review of Psychology* 41: 417–440.

Dunn, Rita, and Kenneth Dunn. 1978. *Teaching Students through Their Individual Learning Styles: A Practical Approach.* Reston, VA: Reston Publishing.

Durodoyle, Beth, and Bertina Hildreth. 1995. "Learning Styles and the African American Student." *Education* 116 (2): 241–71.

Earley, P. Christopher, and Soon Ang. 2003. *Cultural Intelligence: Individual Interactions across Cultures.* Palo Alto, CA: Stanford University Press.

Executive Office of the President. 2014. *Increasing College Opportunity for Low-Income Students: Promising Models and a Call to Action.* January 16. www.whitehouse .gov/sites/default/files/docs/white_house_report_on_increasing_college_ opportunity_for_low-income_students_1-16-2014_final.pdf.

Ferguson, Ronald. 2003. "Teachers' Perceptions and Expectations and the Black-White Test Score Gap." *Urban Education* 38 (4): 460–507.

Gardner, Howard. 1983. *Frames of Mind: The Theory of Multiple Intelligences.* New York: Basic Books.

Gay, Geneva. 2000. *Culturally Responsive Teaching: Theory, Research, and Practice.* New York: Teachers College Press.

Gelfand, Michele J., Lynn Imai, and Ryan Fehr. 2008. "Thinking Intelligently about Cultural Intelligence: The Road Ahead." In *Handbook of Cultural Intelligence*, edited by Soon Ang and Linn Van Dyne, 375–87. Armonk, NY: M. E. Sharpe.

Goddard, Roger, Wayne K. Hoy, and Anita Woolfolk Hoy. 2000. "Collective Teacher Efficacy: Its Meaning, Measure, and Impact on Student Achievement." *American Educational Research Journal* 37 (2): 479–507.

Goodwin, Bryan. 2010/2011. "Research Says . . . Good Teachers May Not Fit the Mold." *Effective Educator* 68 (4): 79–80.

Haberman, Martin. 1995. *Star Teachers of Children in Poverty.* West Lafayette, IN: Kappa Delta Pi.

Hale, Janice E. 2001. *Learning While Black: Creating Educational Excellence for African American Children*. Baltimore: Johns Hopkins University Press.

Hale-Benson, Janice E. 1986. *Black Children: Their Roots, Culture, and Learning Styles*. Rev. ed. Baltimore: Johns Hopkins University Press.

Hall, Edward T. 1976. *Beyond Culture*. New York: Doubleday.

Hilliard, Asa G., III. 1976. *Alternatives to IQ Testing: An Approach to the Identification of Gifted "Minority" Children*. Sacramento, CA: California State Department of Education.

———. 1989. "Teachers and Cultural Styles in a Pluralistic Society." *NEA Today: A Newspaper for Members of the National Education Association* 7 (6): 65–69.

———. 1992. "Behavioral Style, Culture, and Teaching and Learning." *Journal of Negro Education* 61 (3): 370–377.

———. 1995a. *The Maroon within Us*. Baltimore: Black Classic Press.

———. 1995b. "Teacher Education from an African American Perspective." Paper presented at the Annual Meeting of the American Educational Research Association.

———. 1998. *SBA: The Reawakening of the African Mind*. Gainesville, FL: Makare Publishing Company.

———. 2002. *African Power: Affirming African Indigenous Socialization in the Face of the Culture Wars*. Gainesville, FL: Makare Publishing.

Iruka, Iheoma. 2013. "The Black Family: Re-imagining Family Support and Engagement." In *Being Black Is Not a Risk Factor: A Strengths-Based Look at the State of the Black Child*. Washington, DC: National Black Child Development Institute.

Jordan, K. (5 June 2008). "Marva Collins School to Close." WLS-TV Chicago. Retrieved 11 April 2014.

Kise, Jane, and Beth Russell. 2004. "Are They Really Problem Students?" *Principal Leadership* 4 (7): 28–33.

Kohl, Herbert R. 1995. *"I Won't Learn from You": And Other Thoughts on Creative Maladjustment*. New York: New Press.

Kolb, David. 1984. *Experiential Learning: Experience as the Source of Learning and Development*. Upper Saddle River, NJ: Prentice Hall.

Ladson-Billings, Gloria. 1994. *The Dreamkeepers: Successful Teachers of African American Children*. San Francisco: Jossey-Bass.

Lazara, Alex, Joan Danaher, Robert Kraus, and Sue Goode, eds. 2009. *Section 619 Profile*. 16th ed. Chapel Hill, NC: The National Early Childhood Technical Assistance Center.

Lee, Carol D. 2008. "Synthesis of Research on the Role of Culture in Learning among African American Youth: The Contributions of Asa G. Hilliard, III." *Review of Educational Research* 78 (4): 797–827.

Martin, Joanne. 1992. *Cultures in Organizations: Three Perspectives*. Oxford: Oxford University Press.

Myers, Isabel Briggs, Mary H. McCaulley, Naomi L. Quenk, and Allen L. Hammer. 1998. *MBTI® Manual: A Guide to the Development and Use of the Myers-Briggs Type Indicator, 3rd Edition.* Sunnyvale, CA: Consulting Psychologists Press.

Nyborg, Helmuth, ed. 2003. *The Scientific Study of General Intelligence: Tribute to Arthur Jensen.* Amsterdam: Pergamon.

Muijs, Daniel, and David Reynolds. 2002. "Teachers' Belief and Behaviors: What Really Matters?" *Journal of Classroom Interaction* 37 (2): 3–15.

Pang, Valerie, and Velma Sablan. 1998. "How Do Teachers Feel about Their Abilities to Teach African American Students?" In *Being Responsive to Cultural Differences: How Teachers Learn*, edited by Mary E. Dilworth, 39–60. Thousand Oaks, CA: Corwin Press.

Pérez Huber, Lindsay. 2009. "Challenging Racist Nativist Framing: Acknowledging the Community Cultural Wealth of Undocumented Chicana College Students to Reframe the Immigration Debate." Harvard Educational Review 79 (4): 704–29.

Postsecondary National Policy Institute. 2015. *Historically Black Colleges and Universities: A Background Primer.* January 1. www.newamerica.org/postsecondary-national-policy-institute/historically-black-colleges-and-universities-hbcus/.

Roderick, Melissa, Jenny Nagaoka, and Elaine Allensworth (with Vanessa Coca, Macarena Correa, and Ginger Stoker). 2006. *From High School to the Future: A First Look at Chicago Public School Graduates' College Enrollment, College Preparation, and Graduation from Four-year Colleges.* Chicago: University of Chicago Consortium on Chicago School Research.

Rushton, Stephen, Jenni Mariano, and Tary Wallace. 2012. "Program Selection among Pre-Service Teachers: MBTI Profiles within a College of Education." *Creative Education*, 3, 16–23. doi:10.4236/ce.2012.31003.

Schweinhart, Lawrence J., Jeanne Montie, Zongping Xiang, W. Steven Barnett, Clive R. Belfield, and Milagros Nores. 2005. *Lifetime Effects: The HighScope Perry Preschool Study through Age 40.* Ypsilanti, MI: HighScope Press.

Shade, Barbara J. 1982. "Afro-American Cognitive Style: A Variable in School Success?" *Review of Educational Research* 52 (2): 219–44.

———. 1986. "Is There an Afro-American Cognitive Style? An Exploratory Study." *Journal of Black Psychology* 13 (1): 13–16.

Shields, Portia. 1989. "Holy Angels: Pocket of Excellence." *Journal of Negro Education* 58 (2): 203–11.

Society of Saint Pius X. Accessed May 4, 2015. "Marva Collins: Excerpts from *Ordinary Children, Extraordinary Teachers* and *Marva Collins' Way.*" EDOCERE: A Resource for Catholic Education. www.edocere.org/articles/marva_collins.htm.

Stewart, Zakiya M. 2003. *Helping Ordinary Kids Become Extraordinary Learners: Effective Strategies for Closing the Achievement Gap.* Seattle, WA: Black Child Development Institute (BCDI) – Seattle.

U.S. Census Bureau. 2014. "Educational Attainment in the United States: 2014." www.census.gov/hhes/socdemo/education/index.html.

U.S. Department of Education. 1991. *Historically Black Colleges and Universities and Higher Education Desegregation.* January 3. Washington, DC: U.S. Department of Education Office for Civil Rights. www2.ed.gov/about/offices/list/ocr/docs/hq9511.html.

———. 2010. *29th Annual Report to Congress on the Implementation of the Individuals with Disabilities Education Act, 2007.* Washington, DC: Office of Special Education Programs.

U.S. Department of Justice. Office of Juvenile Justice and Delinquency Prevention. 2000. *The High/Scope Perry Preschool Project.* www.ncjrs.gov/pdffiles1/ojjdp/181725.pdf

Vygotsky, L. S. 1978. *Mind in Society: The Development of Higher Psychological Processes.* Cambridge, MA: Harvard University Press.

Watkins, Angela Farris. 2002. "Learning Styles of African American Children: A Developmental Consideration." *Journal of Black Psychology* 28 (1): 3–17.

Willis, Madge Gill. 1989. "Learning Styles of African American Children: A Review of the Literature and Interventions." *Journal of Black Psychology* 16 (1): 47–65.

Wright, Donna Akilah. 2012. "Creating Supportive Learning Environments for African American Learners Using Culture-Based Education." *African American Learners* 1 (2).

York, Darlene Eleanor. 1996. "The Academic Achievement of African Americans in Catholic Schools: A Review of the Literature." In *Growing Up African American in Catholic Schools,* edited by Jacqueline Jordan Irvine and Michéle Foster, 11–46. New York: Teachers College Press.

Yosso, Tara J. 2005. "Whose Culture Has Capital?" *Race Ethnicity and Education* 8 (1): 69–91.

FURTHER READING

Akbar, Na'im. 2004. "The Evolution of Human Psychology for African Americans." In *Black Psychology*, 4th ed., edited by Reginald L. Jones, 99–123. Berkeley, CA: Cobb & Henry.

Collins, Marva. 1992. *Ordinary Children, Extraordinary Teachers.* Hampton Roads, VA: Hampton Roads Publishing.

Collins, Marva, and Civia Tamarkin. 1982. *Marva Collins' Way: Returning to Excellence in Education.* New York: Tarcher/Putnam.

Curenton, Stephanie M., and T. M. Lucus (2007). Assessing Young Children's Oral Narrative Skills: The Story Pyramid Framework. In *Assessment in Emergent and Early Literacy*, edited by Khara L. Pence, 377–427. San Diego: Plural Publishing.

Curenton, Stephanie M., and Tricia A. Zucker. 2013. "Instructional Conversations in Early Childhood Classrooms: Policy Suggestions for Curriculum Standards and Professional Development." *Creative Education* 4 (7A1): 60–68.

Curenton, Stephanie M., Laura M. Justice, Tricia A. Zucker, and Anita S. McGinty. 2013. "Language and Literacy Curriculum and Instruction." In *Handbook of Response to Intervention (RTI) in Early Childhood*, edited by Virginia Buysse and Ellen Peisner-Feinberg, 237–49. Baltimore: Brookes.

Dewey, John. (1938) 1997. *Experience and Education*. New York: Touchstone.

Edwards, Carolyn, Lella Gandini, and George Forman, eds. 1993. *The Hundred Languages of Children: The Reggio Emilia Approach to Early Childhood Education*. Norwood, NJ: Ablex.

Farris-Watkins, Angela. 2002. "Learning Styles of African American Children: A Developmental Consideration." *Journal of Black Psychology* 28 (1): 3–17.

Gadzikowski, Ann. 2013. *Challenging Exceptionally Bright Children in Early Childhood Classrooms*. St. Paul, MN: Redleaf Press.

Irvine, Jacqueline Jordan, ed. 2002. *In Search of Wholeness: African American Teachers and Their Cultural Classroom Practices*. New York: Palgrave Global.

The KIPP Foundation. 2013. *KIPP: 2013 Report Card*.

Kleinfeld, Judith. 1994. "Learning Styles and Culture." In *Psychology and Culture*, edited by Walter J. Lonner and Roy S. Malpass, 151–56. Boston: Allyn and Bacon.

Knowledge Is Power Program (KIPP). 2014. *KIPP: 2014 Report Card*. www.kipp .org/files/dmfile/2014KIPPReportCard.pdf.

Kunjufu, Jawanza. 2011. *Understanding Black Male Learning Style*. Chicago: African American Images.

Ladson-Billings, Gloria. 2001. *Crossing Over to Canaan: The Journey of New Teachers in Diverse Classrooms*. San Francisco: Jossey-Bass.

Malaguzzi, Loris, Marina Castagnetti, Laura Rubizzi, and Vea Vecchi. 1995. *A Journey Into the Rights of Children: As Seen By Children Themselves*. The Unheard Voice of Children Series. Reggio Emilia: Reggio Children Publishing.

Montessori, Maria. 1988. *Dr. Montessori's Own Handbook: A Short Guide to Her Ideas and Materials*. New York: Shocken Books.

———. 2002. *The Montessori Method*. Mineola, NY: Dover Publications.

Ng, Kok-Yee, Linn Van Dyne, and Soon Ang. 2012. "Cultural Intelligence: A Review, Reflections, and Recommendations for Future Research." In *Conducting Multinational Research: Applying Organizational Psychology in the Workplace*, edited by Ann Marie Ryan, Frederick T. L. Leong, and Frederick L. Oswald, 29–58. Washington, DC: American Psychological Association.

Noguera, Pedro. 2007. "Extended View: Race, Student Achievement and the Power and Limitations of Teaching." *Sage Race Relations Abstracts*, 32, 44–47.

Rushton, J. Philippe. 2003. "Race Differences in g and the 'Jensen Effect.'" In *The Scientific Study of General Intelligence: Tribute to Arthur Jensen*, edited by Helmuth Nyborg, 147–86. Amsterdam: Pergamon.

Toney, Aisha, Samantha Brown-Olivieri, Elizabeth Robitaille, and Myrna Castrejon. 2011. *Chartering and Choice as an Achievement Gap-Closing Reform: The Success of California Charter Schools in Promoting African American Achievement*. Sacramento, CA: California Charter Schools Association.

Wilson, Amos. 1991. *Awakening the Natural Genius of Black Children*. New York: Afrikan World Info Systems.

Woodson, Carter Godwin. 1933. *The Mis-Education of the Negro*. Washington, DC: Associated Publishers.

WEBSITES

HighScope Foundation: www.highscope.org

Knowledge Is Power Program (KIPP): www.kipp.org

Seattle Urban Academy: www.sua.org

Urban Preparatory Academy: www.urbanprep.org

ISTJ—the Inspector: www.personalitydesk.com/istj

Diversity, Community, & Achievement. 2011 by Teach for America/Teaching as Leadership: www.teachingasleadership.org

Index

energy, as aspect of cultural intelligence, 67

engagement, disruptive behavior as result of lack of, 3, 88

expectations

of families, 89–90

level in successful programs, 28, 31

of students, 2–3, 90–91

of teachers by third grade, 3

experiential learning model, 138–140

experiential/tactile learning style

Black culture and, 50

described, 37

learning environment based on, 52, 53–54

extraversion (outgoing/energetic vs. solitary/reserved), 42, 43

F

familial capital, 114–115

families

behavioral expectations for students, 106

consultation with, 89–92, 106, 125

homework and, 118–121, 130–131

importance of extended, 114–115

involvement and engagement, 15, 18

meaningful, mutually respectful connection between learning environment and, 83, 132

relationship of successful programs with, 26, 31–32

Feinberg, Mike, 17

fidgeters, 45

"Four Rs" in school culture, 22

G

Gardner, Howard, 36, 38

gender and personality traits, 41

good causes, as curricular element, 21, 86, 133

guardians. *See* families

H

harmony

as element of Black culture, 49

learning environment based on, 53, 56

HighScope

background, 14

benefits for Black children, 140–141

curriculum and pedagogy, 14–16, 26–29, 140

outcomes, 16–17

success of, 135

Hilliard, Asa, 62, 71

Historically Black Colleges and Universities (HBCUs), 14, 26–29

homework, 118–121, 130–131

I

Iceberg Model of culture, 71–72

ideas, sharing with students, 96–98, 126–127

"inattentive" students, 45

individualism in learning environment, 79, 134

information gathering—sensing or intuition (S/N), 40

intelligences. *See* specific types

interactive learning style, described, 37

interdependence/communal, 49, 53

interdependence/spirituality

as element of Black culture, 49–50

learning environment based on, 53, 56

interdisciplinary teams, 18

interpersonal intelligence, described, 38

interpersonal relationships

as element of Black culture, 50

learning environment based on, 53, 56–57

intrapersonal intelligence, described, 38

integrated, connected curriculum, 87
interactive discourse, discussion, and analysis, 78–79, 131
meaningful
  mutually respectful connection to family and community, 83, 132
  mutually respectful teacher-child relationship, 82, 132
  opportunities for connection with nature and each other for higher purpose, good cause, 86, 133
  opportunities for creativity, individualism, and embellishment, 79, 134
  opportunities for self-reflection, 85, 133
  sense of community and belonging, 87, 134
harmony, 53, 56
interdependence/communal, 53
interdependence/spirituality, 53, 56
interpersonal relationships, 53, 56–57
mental challenges, 53, 57–58
physical challenges, 53
realism, 53, 58–59
social environment/visual, 53, 59–60
typical, compared to needs of Black children, 63
verbal intelligence, 53, 60–61
verve/stimulus variety, 53
learning needs
  of Black children compared to typical learning environments, 63
  effects of disconnect with learning environment, 61–62
  meeting, by starting with one culture, 2

student behavior and, 44–46
See also learning styles; multiple intelligences; personality types/traits
learning styles
  ability to articulate, 6
  challenge of diversity of, 2
  existence of Black, 7–8
  incorporating multiple, 35–36
  influence of culture on, 46–47
  types described, 37–38
Levin, Dave, 17
Lifetime Effects: The HighScope Perry Preschool Study through Age 40 (Schweinhart et al.), 16–17, 135
linguistic capital, 114
linguistic/verbal intelligence, described, 39
logical/mathematical intelligence, described, 39

M

mathematical intelligence, described, 39
mediation/conflict resolution process, 15
mental challenges
  as element of Black culture, 50
  in learning environment, 81, 132
  learning environment based on, 53, 57–58
Montessori Method, 135, 141–143
Montie, Jeanne, 16–17, 135
multilayeredness of lives, 52
multiple intelligences
  types described, 38–39
  See also specific types
multiple stimulus, 52
musical/rhythmic intelligence, described, 39
Myers-Briggs Type Indicator (MBTI), 40–41

personality aspects, 44

relationships with families and communities, 121–122

reflective learning style, described, 37

Reggio Emilia approach, 135, 143–145

resistant capital, 115

responsibility

personal, in learning environment, 84, 133

of students for learning, 29

rhetorical questions, 58–59

rhythmic intelligence, described, 39

S

scarcity thinking, 123

schedule of daily activities, 101–105, 128

school-sponsored activities, as curriculum element, 21

Schweinhart, Lawrence J., 16–17, 135

Seattle Urban Academy (SUA), 18–20, 26–28

second/third grades learning environment elements

active, engaged learning, 76–77

collective/collaborative activity and problem solving, 80

competitive mental and physical challenges, 81

educational empowerment/ personal responsibility, 84

examples of integrated, connected curriculum, 87

interactive discourse, discussion, and analysis, 78–79

meaningful

mutually respectful connection to family and community, 83

mutually respectful teacher-child relationship, 82

opportunities for connection with nature and each other for higher purpose, good cause, 86

opportunities for creativity, individualism, and embellishment, 79

opportunities for self-reflection, 85

sense of community and belonging, 87

segregation, 7

self-efficacy, defined, 68

self-reflection, opportunities in learning environment, 85, 133

self-talk, 94

Service Arc, 21

social capital, 115

social development, in successful programs, 28

social environment

learning environment based on, 53, 59–60

obtaining information from, 51

as source of information, 51

social growth and maturity, 19

Socratic method, 24–25

spatial/visual intelligence, described, 39

spiritual capital, 116

spiritual health, 19

spiritualist intelligence, described, 39

spirituality

as element of Black culture, 49–50

learning environment based on, 53, 56

stereotyping, 7, 9, 47

Stewart, Zakiya M., 102, 105

storytelling tradition, 114

students

behavioral expectations of families, 106

characteristics upon starting school, 1

consultations with, to track academic progress, 92